# A Martyr for the Truth

Grazyna Sikorska was born in Katowice in Polish Silesia.

In 1974 she was awarded an MSc degree at the University of Katowice, and came to England to continue her scientific research. For a time she worked with the Polish Catholic émigré weekly *Gazeta Niedzielna*, and in 1979 joined the staff of Keston College, the centre for the study of religion in communist lands, researching all aspects of religious life in her native country.

Grazyna is married to Janusz, whose Polish parents found themselves in England after the war. They met at the Polish Catholic Chaplaincy in London, of which Janusz is President. They have one son, Sławomir, aged two, and live in Kent.

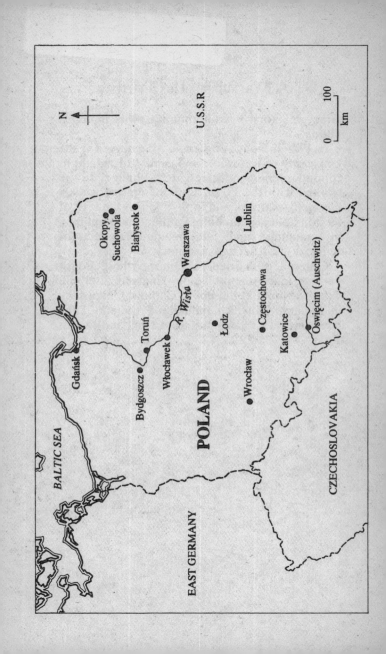

GRAZYNA SIKORSKA

# A Martyr
# for the Truth

Jerzy Popiełuszko

With a Preface by
**Michael Bourdeaux**

**Collins**
**FOUNT PAPERBACKS**

First published by Fount Paperbacks, London in 1985

Copyright © Grazyna Sikorska 1985

Made and printed in Great Britain by
William Collins Sons & Co. Ltd, Glasgow

The photograph of Father Popiełuszko
as a seminarian is the copyright of
Keston College, England © 1984

Keston Book Number 24

This book is dedicated to
my Father
and to the Catholic Poland
that Father Jerzy Popiełuszko
prayed for

# Acknowledgements

I would like to thank:

The many friends of Father Jerzy Popiełuszko in Poland and elsewhere who shall remain nameless;

Marite Sapiets for her suggestions and corrections;

Shirley Harrison for typing the manuscript;

Melanie Ridley, for childminding "on demand";

and my husband, Janusz, without whose help and encouragement this book would never have been written.

I would also like to acknowledge the use of material from issues of *Przeglad Katolicki* (The Catholic Review).

February 1984                                    Grazyna Sikorska

# Contents

# POLISH PRONUNCIATION

For those who want to try pronouncing the Polish names used in this book the following notes may be of interest. The only letter which is different from the English alphabet is the special ł, as in Father Jerzy Popiełuszko's name.

| | | |
|---|---|---|
| Popiełuszko | = | Poppiéwooshco (final o is short as in "of") |
| Wojtyła | = | Voyteewa |
| Wyszynski | = | Visheensky |

| *Polish letter* | | *English pronunciation* |
|---|---|---|
| c | = | ts (usually, though not always!) |
| ch | = | kh (as in lo*ch*) |
| cz | = | ch (as in *ch*ur*ch*) |
| i | = | ee (as in m*ee*t) |
| j | = | y |
| ł | = | w (as in *w*ind) |
| rz | = | zh (as in Geo*rge*) |
| sz | = | sh |
| szcz | = | sh-ch |
| w | = | v |
| y | = | i |

# Preface

In our fraught and tragic century God has many times intervened directly in the affairs of mankind to offer hope to the deprived and the persecuted. Some discern clear signs of the last times, as predicted by Christ at the end of His life. It is hard to read St Matthew Chapter 24 without feeling a resonance in almost every sense which is applicable to the closing years of our century. Verses 9 and 13 predict the Christian martyrs, of whom there have already been more in the twentieth century than in any other. "Then they will deliver you up to tribulation, and put you to death . . . but he who endures to the end will be saved." These words are Christ's assurance to the suffering Church, to a suffering nation and to one of the most recent of His martyrs, Father Jerzy Popiełuszko.

Yet God, faithful to His promises, constantly intervenes in the affairs of mankind. The election of Cardinal Karol Wojtyła as Pope John Paul II, unpredicted and unpredictable, was one of those occasions where God's plan overrode human logic. This event went against the conventional wisdom of hierarchies (of all denominations), it contradicted human caution and the received political views prevalent in so many Christian circles. One part of the *terra incognita* on the spiritual map of Eastern Europe was illuminated by a blinding light of spiritual revelation.

This book rarely mentions the Pope, yet the events it recounts are, in the splendour of Father Jerzy's witness, a direct consequence and extension of that revelation. Yes, there were many more Polish martyrs in the 1940s and in the 1950s than there have been in the 1980s, but equally certainly God is working now in a new way in Poland. And from Poland there is a double message to the world, unpopular though it is in many Christian circles. The author writes of "the evil of the system with its ideology of confrontation, hatred and contempt for man", yet these pages are suffused with the example of Father Jerzy's goodness and integrity.

Not that the book presents an idealized portrait or is an essay in hagiology. Father Jerzy appears as a very human figure with all his weaknesses – but his humanity is transfigured by the role he is called on by God to play. The same could be said of the Polish people as a whole.

Reading these pages, one does feel that the Polish soil is witnessing the epitome of the conflict between good and evil in the world. Peace can never be achieved between north, south, east or west while such injustices remain unresolved. The world can never be safe from the threat of disaster until or unless Poland achieves the right of self-determination.

Finally, Grazyna Sikorska's researches come as near as possible under present conditions to resolving the vexed question: did General Jaruzelski personally authorize the murder? The book presents a picture in which the state apparatus was all working to the same end. Father Jerzy was, after all, the ninety-third victim of similar violence (among them a bishop, several priests and active laymen) since the imposition of martial law. Either the General is not in control of his country or such murders fall into a pattern of official policy, just as they do in neighbouring Lithuania, the only difference there being the screen of greater secrecy provided by the location of that country behind the Soviet frontier.

A friend of Father Jerzy Popiełuszko once said: "A political priest is one who is intimidated by the police and retreats into silence." So here we read of a man whose passionate concern for God and his fellow men led him only in one direction: along the way of the Cross to Calvary.

Michael Bourdeaux
20th February 1985

# 1

# The Catholic Heritage

"Poland's history cannot be understood without Christ. The Polish people cannot be understood without Christ."
(Pope John Paul II, Victory Square, Warsaw, June 1979)

*

"Next to God, for us our first love is Poland. After God we must remain faithful above all to our homeland, to the Polish national culture. We shall love all the people in the world, but only in such an order of priorities.

"And if we see slogans everywhere advocating love for all people and all nations, we do not oppose them; but above all we demand the right to live in accordance with the spirit, history, culture and language of our own Polish land – the unchanged values of our forefathers for centuries."

(Cardinal Stefan Wyszynski, Sermon in St John's Cathedral, February 1974)

*

"The position of the Church will always be the same as the position of the people. The Church means not only the clergy but also the people – those million-strong masses who form the Church; and when the people suffer, when the people are persecuted then the Church shares in their suffering. The mission of the Church is to be with the people every day, to participate in their joys, their sorrows and their sufferings."

(Father Jerzy Popiełuszko, 1984)

*

Poland is a country of paradoxes. Officially it has been part of the "socialist bloc" of East European countries since 1945, when it was surrendered to Soviet domination by the

Western nations – which had originally gone to war to liberate it. Until Solidarity emerged in 1980, the ruling Communist Party claimed some three million members. It is a communist country, where atheism forms an integral part of the Party's political programme, yet where over ninety per cent of all children are baptized, where the words spoken by the head of the Catholic Church carry more weight than those of the Party leader, and where more than once its communist leaders have been forced to turn to the Church for help at times of national crisis. It is a communist country where, especially in rural areas, a local Party boss can often be seen proudly carrying a canopy over the parish priest during the Corpus Christi procession or wholeheartedly singing carols in the church on Christmas Eve. It is a communist country where Mary, the Mother of God, is revered as the Queen of Poland, a country which has given the Universal Church a charismatic and dynamic leader – John Paul II. And it is a country where a genuine workers' movement rebelled against the workers' state, under the banner of the Cross.

If the Soviet Union were to disappear miraculously, if its political system were to be dramatically changed, then communist Poland would collapse overnight. In spite of its official atheism and all the materialistic "re-education" of the Polish people, the country has remained deeply Christian. Catholicism has formed a "national ideology" which has been impervious to communist rule.

In the short history of the "socialist state", the Poles have rebelled against it five times: in 1956, 1968, 1970, 1976 and most recently in 1980 when the ten-million-strong Solidarity Free Trade Union was formed. Although all the revolts failed, each one extended the limits of freedom a little further, the result being another paradox: even when subjected to martial law the Poles were still envied by the other Soviet bloc nations. If the defiant spirit of the Poles has survived so many vicissitudes, including the repression of Solidarity and the accompanying economic hardships and repressions, it is largely due to the unique influence of the Catholic faith. In no other country in Europe, not even in Spain or Ireland, has the Catholic faith achieved such a unique position among the people as a whole or been so strongly identified with national aspirations. A thousand years after the baptism of Poland as a nation the strength of the Polish people still lies in their faith. If the Church were to be removed from Poland's history, nothing would remain – so a Polish archbishop, Teodorowicz, once said. Today, when we often ignore the real existence of spirituality in the life of nations, when we forget their spiritual history, the Archbishop's words might sound naïve. For a Pole they represent an axiom. Every child in Poland knows that Mieszko I of the Piast dynasty married a Christian princess from Bohemia, and that in 966 he and members of his court were baptized. His acceptance of Christianity also marked the beginning of Poland's statehood. The consolidation of the young state was closely related to the process of Christianization. The strong link between the state and the Church was manifested symbolically in the proximity of the king's castle to the cathedral at Wawel in Krakow, and in the Primate of Poland's position as Interrex, who ruled between the death of one monarch and the coronation of the next. It was an important factor in the creation of the Polish national and religious tradition. Despite this bond with the state, the Church has never subordinated itself to the secular authorities or become officially a part of the state, as did the Orthodox Church in Russia, for example. During its long history the Church has not only become the symbol of national identity but also a fearless defender of the people against injustice on the part of oppressive rulers. Struggles between the state authorities and the Church have always been of a moral rather than a political dimension. This tradition goes back as far as 1079, when Bishop Stanisław of Krakow was killed by King Bolesław the Bold for condemning the king's abduction of a peasant woman. Eventually, Stanisław was canonized by the Church and became the patron saint of Poland. Today the

Church sees St Stanisław as one of the first defenders of human rights, although since 1945 Polish history textbooks describe him as a traitor and a rebel.

Mieszko I's choice of Roman rather than Byzantine Christianity brought Poland into the main stream of Western European culture and turned it into an outpost of Catholicism on the eastern borders of Central Europe. Down the centuries, Poland's enemies – Muslim Turks and Tartars, Orthodox Russians, Protestant Swedes and Germans – were all anti-Catholic, so that Poland's wars were fought as a result of threats not only to its nationhood but also to its Catholic religion. Indeed, Poles have always regarded their country as the bastion of Christendom, defending not only itself but also the whole of Christian Europe against constant incursions from the east. Among many "religious" battles fought by the Poles, the most spectacular holds a famous place in European history – the Relief of Vienna. In July 1683 one hundred and thirty-eight thousand Turks, commanded by the Vizier Kara Mustafa, besieged Vienna. The situation was desperate. Responding to an appeal by the Pope and the Emperor of Austria, King Jan Sobieski of Poland immediately proceeded to mobilize, and rapidly led an army of thirty thousand men into Austria. The decisive battle took place on 12th September, and by the evening the immense Ottoman army was in flight; amidst the enthusiastic acclamations of a populace delivered from its great sufferings, the King of Poland entered the gates of Vienna as its saviour. It is a tragic irony that King Jan Sobieski's victory saved the same state which a hundred years later shared in the partition of the Polish Republic.

If the Relief of Vienna is the battle best known outside Poland, then the Battle of Warsaw in 1920 is by far the most important to every Pole. Only two years before, in November 1918, Poland had regained its independence after over one hundred and twenty years of being partitioned between the three neighbouring states: Russia, Prussia and Austria. Despite Lenin's pre-revolutionary assurances that the Poles should be free to determine their own fate, the aggressive Bolshevik state attacked Poland, hoping to spread the Russian Revolution to the rest of Europe ("over the dead body of the Polish State" as the Soviet war slogan pronounced). The young and badly equipped Polish army was rapidly losing the war, and in August the battle front stopped just outside Warsaw. As the decisive battle in which the Soviet army was defeated took place on 15th August – the Marian Feast of the Assumption – it was and still is considered a miraculous victory of Christianity over God's Marxism.

In the sixteenth century the Reformation – the only other serious threat to Catholicism in the past – reached Poland. A part of the Polish nobility soon espoused Protestantism but the masses remained Catholic, as did the king. At the time when Europe was being shattered by civil wars over religion, the Polish king – renowned as a man of tolerance – was being urged by the Catholics to take action against the Protestant heretics. He refused however, saying, "I am not the ruler of your conscience." Within two generations, the Counter-Reformation regained the allegiance of most Protestant Poles, and since then no challenge from the Protestant West or the Orthodox East has made much of a dent in Polish loyalty to the Apostolic See. Unlike in the rest of Europe, the Counter-Reformation did not set up an inquisition or burn heretics. In fact, after 1572 the elected Polish monarchs promised in their coronation oaths to uphold the right of their citizens to freedom of worship. Thanks to this relative tolerance Poland gained a reputation as "asylum hereticorum". More importantly the Roman Catholic Church did not acquire a negative image among Poles.

At the end of the eighteenth century the Polish Republic was partitioned amongst its three neighbours, Austria, Russia and Prussia, and for one hundred and twenty-three years the Polish state disappeared from the map of Europe. Along with the entire population, the Church was repressed by the occupying powers, particularly Russia and Prussia. Ruthless Russification and Germanization went hand in hand with persecution of the Catholic Church and attempts to "convert" Poles to Orthodoxy and Lutheranism. In the Russian zone of partition, the Church was additionally persecuted for the support it gave to the two national Polish uprisings in 1830 and 1863. On the Tsar's orders, some forty-seven monastic orders were then dissolved, ten bishops were exiled from their dioceses, and many priests were killed or exiled. Their common suffering brought the Church and the Polish people closer together, and the identification of Polishness and Catholicism was reaffirmed and strengthened. Across the partitioning borders, the Church and the Catholic faith became the most important link in maintaining the Polish nationhood. The Church kept Poland spiritually together at a time when it was politically divided.

The Polish Catholic Church also shared the tragic fate of its people during the Second World War, at the hands of both the Germans and the Russians. In the first few days of the war some five hundred priests from the two Polish dioceses of Chelmno and Wtocław were shot dead by the Germans. Hundreds of nuns were arrested and imprisoned in a special camp. Many were later sent to Ravensbruck concentration camp, some were shot. According to church historians, one thousand nine hundred and ninety-six priests, four bishops, two hundred and thirty-eight nuns, one hundred and seventy monks, and one hundred and thirteen seminarians perished in German concentration camps between 1939 and 1945.[1]

The most trying time for the Church and for the Catholic faith of the Polish people came, however, with the imposition of a communist regime after the Second World War. The new system, introduced "in the name of the working class and for the good of the whole nation", soon revealed its totalitarian face. This system, which proclaimed a kind of new eschatology and the creation of a heaven on earth as being almost within reach, soon proved to be a political doctrine which aimed not only at the nationalization of the means of production but also of every sphere of life, including that of individual thought. All that might escape total Party control was to be destroyed. Human rights and the dignity of man became suddenly subordinated to the state and history. The Party's monopoly over the media and the education system cut people off from the values of truth, history and tradition, and from their roots, above all those of Christian culture. Through the state monopoly over the economy, the people were forced into dependence upon the state for the necessities of life; which in turn made the people easier to manipulate. Most tragically, a reign of terror was established by the extensive security system. In this way a perfect model of enslavement came about, whose two supporting pillars were lies and fear. There was no place in "socialist" Poland for the Church, with its transcendental vision of man. However, if the Communists found it impossible to destroy the Church and its "opium of the people"; if the Party found it impossible to re-educate the Polish people in "scientific Marxism", it was not only because of the Catholic Church's organizational structure. It was mainly because in fighting against religion the Communists were fighting the national consciousness, the Polishness inextricably bound to Christian tradition. Secularization and atheism were seen and felt by the Poles as Sovietization, a new form of captivity.

The state has never reconciled itself to the position of the Catholic Church amongst the Poles, even during the short times of *rapprochement* between the two. The state has constantly attempted, if not to destroy the Church then at least to limit its influence, or to use it as a subservient tool to uphold the internal peace of Poland. Although persecution has never reached the level of that in Czechoslovakia or the Soviet Union, the Church in Poland has had its share of painful experiences: nine bishops, including the Primate, Cardinal Stefan Wyszynski, and some nine hundred priests suffered imprisonment in the

1950s; the Church was deprived of access to the media and of the right to form Catholic associations, and many of its properties have been confiscated, including a thousand charitable institutions (known under one name as CARITAS). Those who openly manifested their faith were harassed and discriminated against in their professional careers. Volumes could be written about the daily battle of the Church against state harassment over the last forty years. There have been innumerable examples of the struggle for religious instruction in schools, for the right to hang a crucifix on a classroom wall, for permission to build churches and catechetical centres, for freedom to hold religious processions and pilgrimages, for a Catholic press and Catholic literature, for the right to work with young people and to organize public Christian cultural events.

The Catholic Church has played an essential role in the Poles' struggle for freedom and human dignity, always setting itself against the absolute claims to power made by the communist state, and appealing instead to the higher laws and values of God-given morality, unmasking the system's falsehood, condemning injustice and demanding reforms. It has never called for revolution, yet it has mobilized the populace and fought against compromise and the feeling of hopelessness. Through the Church's own "mass media" – the pulpits in over twelve thousand churches and some twenty thousand religious instruction centres within the "illegal" Light-Life renewal movement (which in the past fifteen years has involved three hundred thousand young Poles) plus the numerous festivals of faith dedicated to the Virgin Mary – the Church has preached its vision of man: created for freedom as a child of God. Over the years there has been formed a Polish attitude to faith which has made it the immediate support and natural basis for daily life, and the preferred solution for people's most important problems. While the communist ideology has gradually become less and less influential, Christianity has emerged as the "alternative ideology". Since 1970 few people have seriously spoken of "socialist ideals". Instead material well-being on the level enjoyed by people in the West was the communist goal put forward by the newly appointed Party leader. From official addresses at that time it seemed as if there was no greater problem facing the Polish Communists than to secure a car for every Polish family. However, within a decade the Polish economic miracle turned into a total catastrophe, leaving the country on the verge of bankruptcy. At a time when the purchase of a pair of shoes – let alone a car – has become a major crisis for the average household budget, even the economic argument for the leading role of the Party has disappeared. Today the last argument remaining is the Soviet tank and the Party's hopes that the fate of Hungary in 1956 and Czechoslovakia in 1968 are still vivid in people's memories.

But even any remaining fear was dispelled on 16th October 1978 when a Polish Cardinal, Karol Wojtyła, became the first Polish Pope to lead the Universal Church. His elevation to the See of St Peter was seen as God's reward given to the Polish nation for its faithfulness to Christ and His Church, symbolizing the victory of Christ over totalitarian evil. The Pope's pilgrimage to his native country in June 1979 united the whole nation. The millions of Poles who during his visit manifested their faith peacefully and with dignity proved the complete bankruptcy of communist ideology in Poland. The Polish Pope reminded the Polish workers that, "Christ will never accept that man should be seen or see himself as a mere means of production." "He hung on the cross to protest against any degradation of man, including degradation through work." He left his fellow countrymen with a clear message: "Do not be afraid to insist on your rights. Refuse a life based on lies and double thinking. Do not be afraid to suffer with Christ." Within a year of Pope John Paul II's pilgrimage, the ten-million-strong trade union movement "Solidarity" had been formed in Poland.

Many observers who, in August 1980, saw on the gates of the Gdansk shipyard religious banners with pictures of the Madonna and the Polish Pope, or who saw the faces of workers in overalls kneeling in the open air to receive communion, could make no sense of these scenes. The Polish workers' revolution, however, cannot be explained exclusively in economic or even political terms, for the Solidarity movement was in essence a spiritual revolution, founded above all in response to the violations of human dignity and human rights, and carried out in a Christian spirit. At the centre of this national protest movement was the spiritual value of the truth. The Solidarity revolution was a protest against falsehood, against the total untruthfulness of the communist system. Deeply rooted, if not always clearly formulated, in the consciousness of the striking and struggling masses, was the intuitive conviction that a person is free when he bears witness to the truth which he knows and acknowledges. The Soviet system of enslavement, which is based above all on lies, awakened in them a deep yearning for liberation through the truth. This yearning became so strong in the few years prior to August 1980, that the example of the shipworkers in Gdansk immediately inspired the entire nation to break down the barriers of fear. Fear is the second most important support of the Soviet system, fear which does not allow people to bear witness to the truth or to demand their rights. In 1980 the Polish people recognized and experienced the way to liberation, the way to true human freedom, by overcoming fear and bearing witness to the truth.

At the centre of this Polish revolution was also another value, expressed symbolically by the Cross. It was a deep conviction motivated by faith, a conviction that there is meaning in suffering for the truth and even sacrificing one's life for it: that the victory of resurrection can be achieved only through the Cross. The Cross also conveyed another essential concept: the idea of a struggle for liberation without hatred or the use of violence, and with a readiness to forgive.[2] In countless moments of tension the Polish workers did not allow themselves to be provoked into bloody confrontations. On many occasions the leaders of

Solidarity warned against the use of violence and terrorism, openly stating their readiness to forgive and their willingness, should those who dictate show signs of goodwill, to change course and begin a dialogue. It is an extraordinary fact that in the sixteen tense and passionate months of Solidarity's "above-ground" existence no one was killed. Solidarity was not a peace movement as such, but it was unquestionably peaceful and non-violent.

A tape which found its way to the West, in the winter of 1982, records an incident at the Wujek coal mine in Silesia, during the first days of martial law. ZOMO riot police were ordered to crush the resistance of the miners who had barricaded themselves inside the mine. In one of the encounters between riot police and the miners a few policemen were captured. They were put – ad hoc – "on trial", and found guilty of many atrocities. While the miners were arguing over the punishment, one man stood up and reminded the rest of the Mass they had participated in earlier that day, and of the communion so many of them had received. "Can we take vengeance on these people, with Christ in our hearts?" he asked. Later the policemen, undoubtedly very happy yet absolutely stunned, were released unharmed. It only adds to the tragedy that, on the imposition of martial law, the first people to lose their lives were the miners from the same Wujek colliery, shot by armed police.

Since then the number of known victims of the "return to law and order" in Poland has steadily grown, and on 30th October 1984, when Father Jerzy Popiełuszko's body was found, the running total reached ninety-three. Significantly, on the very same day that Father Jerzy was kidnapped on the highway from Bydgoszcz to Warsaw, in Lublin Stanisław Chac, one of Solidarity's local leaders, disappeared. He was found the next day lying in the street with signs of having been tortured. He died on 21st October without regaining consciousness. The death of these two young Poles, a priest and a Solidarity member, became a symbolic reminder of the common fate of the

11

Church and its people. Despite the absence of any hope for political change, the Polish people's opposition to totalitarian mendacity and coercion has remained unshaken. This opposition is based on a moral rather than a political revulsion against a way of life which forces people to conceal their true selves.[3] The religious faith of the Poles makes it difficult for them to live a life of compulsory pretence and impossible for them to accept the "socialist" vision of man – which limits him to being "the means of production". This same belief prevents them from giving up hope. The present Primate of Poland, Cardinal Jozef Glemp, once said: "No handcuffs, no regulations, no repression, no enforced emigration can destroy the ideals of our nation. They exist in its soul."

1 *Historia Koscioka*, Father Josef Uminski.
2 "A theology of liberation – In the Spirit", Father Franciszek Blachnicki, *Religion in Communist Lands* Vol. 12, No. 2.
3 This practice of Ketman, leading an inner and outer life, to think only what one feels and say what one is expected to say, is vividly described in a book by the Polish Nobel laureate, Czesław Miłosz, entitled *The Captive Mind*.

# 2

# The Early Years

The first thing that struck anybody who came across Father
Jerzy Popiełuszko, even during a brief encounter, was his
gentleness – his inner harmony and almost boyish
innocence could be seen in his eyes. But after only a few
sentences had been exchanged it became clear that this
gentle and modest priest was also a man of stalwart will,
courage and determination. By the time they left Father
Jerzy, people would already have an image of him as an
uncompromising follower of Christ and a great Polish
patriot.

Jerzy was a true son of Podlasie, a region of eastern
Poland little known even among Poles themselves. From
a small hill which used to stand on the outskirts of Jerzy's
home village of Okopy, but which has now been flattened,
one could see the eastern border of Poland. Beyond it
begin the almost infinite lands of the Soviet Union,
Poland's powerful neighbour. However, it is here too, in
the little town of Suchowola, just a few yards from the
church were Jerzy was baptized and four kilometres from
Okopy, that a huge stone, bearing an appropriate
inscription, marks the centre of Europe.

The local people are peaceful and friendly. This may be
due to the calming influence of the largest lowland forest
in Europe, as well as the people's work on the land. These
people are, however, also hardened by many historical
trials, stalwart in their attachment to their Polish
nationality and to Catholicism. Until the Second World
War these lands were a real national and religious
hotchpotch, with a population including Catholics of both
the Latin and Eastern Rites, Protestants (especially

Calvinists), Orthodox Christians, Jews and even some Muslims. In Suchowola, in addition to the Catholic church building, there also used to be a wooden synagogue dating from the seventeenth century, but this was destroyed by the Germans. Not far away in Kruszyniany the Muslims had a mosque, which still stands to this day. In another small town called Orli there was a prominent Calvinist centre. It is to this hotchpotch that many attribute the local high standard of hospitality, unique even by Polish standards. Dispersed among other nationalities and religions, the local Poles used to consider every meeting, even a chance encounter, as an important event calling for a generous, almost unending celebration. Father Jerzy was a typical son of Podlasie in this respect – warm and welcoming, with a sense of hospitality which grew into a legend during his lifetime.

The people of Podlasie found it particularly difficult to reconcile themselves to the new post-war Poland. All the political changes came from the East, and this was enough for them to be seen as hostile, anti-Polish and anti-Catholic. These strong anti-Russian feelings had their origins in the times of the partitions, when the region had become part of the Tsarist Empire. The aggressive Russification of those days, and the ruthless struggle against Catholicism and the Catholic Church, did not pass Podlasie by, but despite all the persecutions the people remained faithful to their national identity and to their religion. This is a land of martyrs for the faith, especially among the Eastern Rite Catholics (Uniates). The 1874 Cossack massacres of crowds at prayer in the villages of Drelow and Pratulin are still alive in popular memory. The local people took an active part in the two anti-Russian uprisings of the nineteenth century. For over six months in the period 1830–31 a Polish partisan army fought the Russians in the nearby forests. In the January uprising of 1863 some seventy-five per cent of the equivalent secondary school pupils in Białystok took part. The Podlasians had to pay for their patriotism with the destruction of three villages, burnt down and ploughed over by the Russians; all their inhabitants, as well as many others, were sent to Siberia. In 1864 the parish of Karpowicze was abolished and merged with Suchowola. The church was demolished and transported to a different village, where it was rebuilt as an Orthodox church.

In 1812 the local people welcomed Napoleon's army, especially the Polish legions within it, as it marched towards Moscow on the nearby old merchant road to the east, which dated from the early eighteenth century. In 1920 the Bolshevik army used the same road to enter Poland. In Białystok, a Polish communist government headed by Feliks Dzierzynski (a leading Polish Communist and founder of today's KGB) was only awaiting news of the Bolshevik victory of the Polish army at the battle outside Warsaw on 15th August, before moving to the capital – news that never came. During the Second World War the local populace gave every possible support to the very active underground partisan army in this region. In the one small forest of Nowosiotki lie the bodies of over four thousand people, including priests and nuns, killed by the Germans as the price for this support.

After the war these people witnessed an arbitrary shift of the Polish eastern borders, by which nine-tenths of the territory of the diocese of Wilno (Vilnius) was lost to the newly enlarged Soviet Union. The archbishop of the diocese of Wilno, Romuald Jalbrzykowski, was forced to leave his bishopric and moved back behind the new border to Białystok. The people of Okopy and Suchowola considered themselves very lucky to be on the Polish side of the border, as the USSR was now just twenty kilometres away. However, they could not forget that over a million Poles, who simply happened to live further east, had been forced into Soviet citizenship.

It was against this background and historical tradition that on 14th September 1947, in the small village of Okopy, Jerzy Popiełuszko was born into the peasant family of Marianna and Władysław Popiełuszko. This was the year when, in accordance with the Yalta agreements between Stalin and the Western Allies, there took place an election which was supposed to decide democratically the political future of Poland. This election was carried out in an atmosphere of political murder, blackmail and terror which resembled the darkest days of the German occupation. Even then, the final results had to be virtually manufactured to prove to the world that the Poles themselves had chosen the new path of communist development. In fact Poland's fate had already been sealed two years before, when the Soviet Red Army "liberated" the country from German occupation. If the Poles found it difficult to be grateful it was because the price they had to pay was almost unbearable: a new Soviet occupation and a communist, Godless system against which they had already successfully defended themselves once, only twenty-five years earlier.

Jerzy Popiełuszko was thus a contemporary of communist Poland. He was one of the generation in which the Polish Communist Party put all its hope, for it was a generation untouched by the pre-war "capitalist" system and "religious indoctrination". His was the generation which, according to the plans drawn up by the Communists, was to be brought up in a new Godless way to produce a new communist man as well as a new Godless Polish nation. In this respect Father Jerzy's biography is also the story of Polish communism so far.

Only two days after his birth, like the majority of Polish infants, Jerzy was baptized in the parish church of St Peter and Paul in Suchowola, and was given the name Alfons after his godfather, a name he used throughout his childhood. Allegedly it was Cardinal Wyszynski who persuaded him to change the name when he entered the Warsaw Seminary, since he felt that Alfons was a name often used in popular folk songs to describe someone of questionable repute and was therefore not suitable for a priest. Thus a new man – Jerzy Popiełuszko – came into being.

Jerzy's parents are neither rich nor poor. They own a few hectares of fertile land and some cows. Their standard of living has never been high. Even today the house has no modern sanitation, and water has to be drawn from a well. The modest two-roomed house has only recently been slightly enlarged to provide accommodation for the Popiełuszkos' youngest son and his wife, Danuta. In Jerzy's childhood, during wintertime the whole family used to sleep in his parents' room, as that contained the one huge stove, which took up an entire wall and provided the necessary heating.

Marianna and Władysław had to work hard to provide for their five children: three sons and two daughters. Of these Jadzia died in her infancy, leaving Teresa as the oldest, then Joseph, Jerzy and finally the youngest, Stanisław. Out of the four children only Stanisław remained in Okopy, and he still lives in his parents' house, together with his wife.

"Jadzia was an extraordinary child", recalls Marianna Popiełuszko. "She was only a year and ten months old when she died, yet she prayed better than the older children. She knew the 'Our Father' and the Creed by heart. On Christmas Eve Jadzia asked for a Christmas wafer, shared it with us and died peacefully. The first of my children offered up to God . . . After Jadzia it was Jerzy who was different from my other children. So patient, so persevering . . . When he was born his whole tiny body was covered with yellowish ulcers. The doctor said this was as a result of my working too hard during pregnancy. But he never complained or cried, he put his little finger into his mouth and looked at me so understandingly . . . he always endured suffering so well, he never complained . . . always smiling, always contented . . ."

Jerzy's life, like that of other peasant boys, was hard. He was expected to put in his share of work at home and in the fields, after school and during his holidays. There was also very little time for his parents to share their affection with all the children, but Jerzy grew up with a deep respect for his mother and father and loved them dearly. Even as a priest Jerzy often liked to visit his parents. He would usually arrive hurricane fashion, with time only for a cup of tea, and after kissing his mother's hands and embracing his father he would disappear, carrying with him a loaf of home-made bread and some home-made sausage.

The Popiełuszko family, like most other families in the region, were devout, practising Catholics, who took their faith very seriously and made every effort to pass it on to their children. The parish church, as well as Jerzy's school, was in Suchowola, some four kilometres from Okopy. Yet from his very first communion, every morning at seven o'clock Jerzy was in the church serving as altar boy during the Mass celebrated by the parish priest. Jerzy did not see this as a sacrifice, however, but treated his service very naturally as the normal duty of a Catholic boy. The fact that the parish priest regarded him as the best altar boy was not due to any competitiveness on his part, far from it. Jerzy's attitude, developed in early childhood, which he himself summarized in one of his last interviews, was: "Whatever I undertake, I try to do it well or not at all. I try to put my whole heart into it or I just leave it." Joseph, Jerzy's elder brother, recalls the opinion of Jerzy held by their parish priest some thirty years ago, "Whatever this boy decides to do in the future, he will do it well." Joseph recalls another incident which at the time shocked everyone. Jerzy was then eight or nine years old, and his brothers and sister were making little figures out of chestnuts. Somehow a nail pierced Jerzy's hand. He just clenched his fist and didn't say a word. It was only some time later that one of the children noticed blood pouring from his hand and told their parents.

On 17th June 1956, when he was nine years old, Jerzy received the sacrament of Confirmation from the diocesan auxiliary bishop and chose the name of Kazimierz – the patron of the diocese of Wilno.

In 1961 Jerzy finished the seventh grade of his primary school and entered the local secondary school in

Suchowola, which had been established only after the war and gave the local peasant boys a great opportunity to learn and develop. It even had a kind of "hall of residence" for children from faraway villages. Significantly, the school was founded as early as 1945 by a young and dedicated priest, Father Kazimierz Wilczewski, with the enthusiastic support of Father Stefan Porczyk, then parish priest of Suchowola. The school owes most, however, to its local teachers. They soon proved not only to have excellent pedagogical qualifications but also to be both patriotic and religious. In effect therefore this rural school had an academic standard equal to the best schools in the country, which accounts for the unusually high proportion of its pupils who went on to university. It was though perhaps more important that, at a time when Polish schools were being run along the lines of communist internationalism, in the Suchowola school Jerzy and his friends were being brought up in a Polish and Catholic tradition.

It was at school that Jerzy learnt the true history of Poland and his own region; and it was there that his religious convictions matured. There was not a single teacher on the staff who was not a practising Catholic, and this made an enormous impression on the pupils. From this small town of Suchowola some thirty-seven boys have been ordained as priests in the last forty years. Jerzy is remembered by his teachers as a "middling but ambitious pupil", who was never very good at sciences but had a talent for more humanistic subjects. When he left he received distinctions in history and Russian. He also liked Polish literature. One of his former teachers still remembers Jerzy as "a modest, truthful child, always ready to help others" but also one with a very inquisitive mind – always searching for the truth.

His decision to become a priest matured silently and in solitude. At school he was rather a loner and never took to crowds. He used to leave home an hour before the other children and walked to school alone – there were so many matters he had to think about, as he explained to his friends. In the end his tendency to analyse all problems from a moral and ethical perspective won him the name of "philosopher". He was not one to talk about himself, a characteristic that remained with him throughout his life. When asked a personal question he would give a short and courteous reply, as if he did not want to waste any of the time which could be used in listening to others – which he always did gladly. Jerzy broke the news of his intention to enter the Seminary on the day of his graduation dance. Although it took everyone by surprise no one was really astonished, for in everyone's opinion, and especially in that of those who knew him well, Jerzy had been developing naturally towards the priesthood since his early childhood. According to his brother, Joseph, some credit for Jerzy's vocation should go to their grandmother Marianna, a religious woman who had an enormous influence on the whole Popiełuszko family.

Jerzy decided to enter the Warsaw Seminary against the advice of the parish priest, who suggested a local one in Białystok. The level of vocations was always very high in that part of Poland, and over-subscribed to the available places, so a certain number of entrants would prepare for the priesthood in seminaries in other districts. Amongst the seminaries, the one in Warsaw seemed to be the most popular. Local boys who were already studying in Warsaw used to spend their holidays at home, and it was their enthusiastic stories which stimulated the others, among them probably Jerzy. His mother recalls the number of times she saw Jerzy talking to a Warsaw seminarian while he was grazing the cows. She could never understand what her little son, then still in primary school, could find in common with a wise cleric. According to Jerzy's mother, he chose the Warsaw Seminary because of its proximity to Niepokalanow (The Place of the Immaculate One) – a Franciscan friary created by Father Maximilian Kolbe, the Polish saint who gave his life for another prisoner in the concentration camp at Auschwitz. It was Jerzy's "most loved place in the whole world". He visited Niepokalanow often, and persuaded his family and friends to accompany him. All his life Father Jerzy remained under the great influence of Father Maximilian Kolbe, who was his hero. To Father Jerzy, Saint Maximilian was a symbol of the victory of a man who, despite being enslaved by force, remained spiritually free. All his life Father Jerzy tried to follow Saint Maximilian's credo: "In order to remain spiritually free men, we must live in the truth."

On 24th June 1965 Jerzy entered the Warsaw Seminary of John the Baptist, where for the next seven years he prepared himself intellectually and spiritually for ordination into the priesthood. It was a year in which the Polish Church was about to celebrate its first Millennium, but which also marked the height of an anti-Church campaign and saw the worst Church-state relations since the early 1950s. By using blackmail and pressure on the weaker priests, the authorities tried to split the Church and to create a schismatic national Catholic Church. At the same time, every "legal" means was used to restrict the Church's freedom of action. After banning religious instruction in schools, the authorities tried to extend their control over the teaching of religion in parish buildings and even in private homes. People who accommodated such classes were harassed and discriminated against. No building permission was granted for new churches in expanding towns. Religious publications were kept to a minimum, and books for children were almost unobtainable. The Polish mass media carried on a vicious and slanderous campaign against the Primate of Poland, Cardinal Wyszynski. Attempts were made to split the Polish Episcopate, and foreign travel was severely restricted for Polish clergy. Heavy taxes were imposed on church property; seminaries were taxed as if they were luxury hotels. Seminarians were called up into the army despite an agreement giving them exemption, and after only a year in the Seminary Jerzy found himself doing two years of military service in one of the three special "clerical" units, in Bartoszyce. The other two were in

Szczecin on the Baltic coast, and Brzeg on the river Odra. At first Jerzy's mother greatly feared that her son might be forced to change his vocation because of intimidation. But when she had a dream in which she was told that "God always looks after those whom He has chosen", her despair evaporated.

The history of the special units for seminarians goes back to the late 1950s. At first seminarians were dispersed among the ordinary units, but soon this practice was abandoned as they had an important influence on the religious faith of the ordinary soldiers. An attempt to send seminarians into special units for men with criminal records also failed. It was then that plans for special "clerical" units were drawn up. The units were directly under the command of the Ministry of Defence, or rather of its political headquarters. Officers were very carefully selected for their ideological "purity", and every unit always had a handful of lay soldiers who, by a strange coincidence, consisted solely of the most eager young communist activists. The whole idea was one of political indoctrination. The scheme was, however, doomed from the start – the seminarians proved on the whole to be better prepared for discussion of the virtues and flaws of the two world-views, the religious and the materialistic. Often they simply ignored the lecturer and used the time to study theological textbooks hidden under their desks.

Conscription was seen by the authorities as a convenient method of punishing the most outspoken bishops. It was from their dioceses that the greatest percentage of seminarians was called up. Several priests from Pope John Paul II's diocese of Krakow, who once served in the Polish army, recall how the then Cardinal Wojtyła stressed, during the meetings they had with him, that he felt personally responsible for the "calling up" of the clerics. He was convinced that they were being punished for his firm attitude towards the state authorities.

Military service was also used in an effort to break the seminarians psychologically. Different types of harassment were tried, from forbidding common prayer to attempts at forcing the weakest individuals into co-operation with the authorities. This harassment was the seminarians' first experience of the difficulties they would shortly be facing as Catholic priests, and their first test of courage and adherence to the faith.[1] Jerzy was not exempt from such harassment. One day he was found by an officer with a rosary in his hand and was promptly ordered to throw it down and trample on it: "If you will not tread on the rosary then I will tread on you", he was told. He refused. He was severely beaten and locked in the punishment cell for a month. As Jerzy always tried to spare his parents, they only learnt of this many years later. In another incident he refused to take off his religious medallion. Ironically, it was in those special units that Jerzy and his colleagues learnt to overcome fear: an experience which was supposed to break the seminarians backfired and strengthened them instead. It was at this time that Jerzy also lost his respect for the communist Polish army.

He returned to Warsaw in 1968 and soon after had to undergo a serious operation on his thyroid gland. After that his bouts of illness never really ceased, although he himself tried to play down the bad state of his health. It was partly due to his own illness that Jerzy was so sensitive towards the sufferings of others. In the Seminary he always cared for others, whilst at the same time managing to find people in need of help in the town. For even then Jerzy understood his apostolate in a very definite way – the way taught to him in the Warsaw Seminary. He was primarily to carry out his mission through action, using words only as a helpful aid. To this form of apostolate he remained faithful until his death.

1 *Spotkania* (Encounters) No. 10, 1980.

# 3

# The Challenge of Priesthood

On 28th May 1972 Jerzy was ordained a priest by Cardinal Stefan Wyszynski, Primate of Poland. His first post was in the parish of Zabki, just outside Warsaw, where he soon began to make his presence felt in parish life. The parish priest of Zabki, Father Tadeusz Karolak, still remembers him as a man with an unusually strong sense of duty, which drove him to work far beyond the limits of his frail health. This sense of duty remained one of the most outstanding features of his ministry. Another feature was the affection and respect he always enjoyed among children and young people wherever he went. Jerzy had a great influence on them: they admired the harmony of Father Jerzy's preaching with his life. He never tried to impose his religious conviction by force, he never theorized or moralized. He was bringing them closer to religion and to God through the work he was doing for others. Through his life he showed them the meaning of the Christian way of life. There was only one thing that Father Jerzy would not tolerate, and that was the condemnation of other people, however bad they appeared to be. "Do not judge," he would always say, "God will judge them."

In Zabki, apart from the usual work of a young assistant priest in a busy parish – saying Mass, hearing confessions, visiting sick and troubled people at home, holding catechism classes for children and teenagers, conducting funerals and so on – Jerzy soon began a rosary circle for young people. The circle was not just a prayer group, it was more a group where young people learnt the meaning of Christian witness in everyday life. These youngsters, for example, influenced by Father Jerzy, began to collect various gifts and useful items, which every few weeks they would take to the kindergarten. Father Jerzy used to spend most of his free moments in the nearby hospital and quickly became a familiar figure, welcomed by both patients and staff.

Young Polish priests are expected to gain experience in several parish communities before they settle down on their own as parish priests. In October 1975, after three years in Zabki, Father Jerzy was transferred to the parish of "the Mother of God, Queen of Poland" in Anin, another Warsaw suburb. He spent three more years there, and in May 1978 was promoted and moved to the parish of "the Infant Jesus" in Zoliborz, a workers' district of Warsaw. Father Jerzy's final parish of St Stanisław Kostka is in the same district. He immersed himself unreservedly in parish work, as he had done in Zabki and Anin, and soon became a favourite among children and young people. His ill health, however, combined with his frenzied work rate, soon began to take its toll. One day Father Czesław, another young priest working in the parish, was sitting in a confessional box whilst Father Jerzy was celebrating Mass. He noticed that Father Jerzy's voice was weakening – then suddenly it stopped. Father Czesław looked out to see Jerzy lying at the altar, unconscious. A local doctor, Barbara Janiszewska, was summoned and came immediately. For the only time in his life Father Czesław, although feeling shaky and uncertain, had to finish the Mass begun by another priest.

Later Jerzy spent a long time in the Institute of Haematology in Warsaw. He tried to hide his ill health as much as he could, but it was apparent to everyone that Father Jerzy did not have enough strength to carry out his parish commitments – especially as he found it impossible to rest unless he was certain that all parish matters were being attended to. As he could never be sure of this he always worked on until he was totally exhausted. To ease his work load, after only one year at the Infant Jesus parish Father Jerzy was moved to the academic church of St Anna

– a "parish" church for all Warsaw students. He was put in charge of the "medical group", the students of medicine. He brought new life to the group and soon it became one of the most active within the Warsaw academic community. He organized lectures, discussions, retreats and summer camps, and was always available to listen to their problems, offering his advice if asked. When Father Jerzy left St Anna's church in May 1980 the group was so attached to him that they simply followed him to his new church, that of St Stanisław Kostka. By that time the members of this group, like all the others he had taken spiritual care of, had been transformed into his close friends. Among all these groups, however, the medical group was the one for which he had developed a special affection.

Despite all the other duties he had to carry out in the last years of his short life, he always found time not only to hold prayer meetings, but to celebrate regular Masses for the students in the hall just outside his room, at St Stanisław Kostka parish house, on the third Saturday of each month. He also found time for informal chats – he seemed to know the problems of everyone in the group and was ready to come to their aid in any crisis. He was with the students during both the strikes at the Medical Academy, in the spring and autumn of 1981, cooling down hot-heads but also keeping their spirits high.

From 1979 onwards, another group of friends began to form around Father Jerzy. At the end of 1978, Cardinal Wyszynski had appointed him chaplain to the nurses of Warsaw, and as part of his ministry he was expected to celebrate a special Mass for them in the Res Sacra Miser Chapel, close to the church of St Anna in the famous old-town district of Warsaw. When Jerzy went to say his first Mass there he found that there was only one woman in the church, and even she was not a nurse. He was heartbroken. Soon after he was invited to attend an annual Christmas "Opołatek" – the traditional and symbolic breaking and sharing of wafer bread – given by Cardinal Wyszynski in the

Primate's residency. There he met a few nurses and told them sadly about the Mass with no participants. The nurses explained that for several years hardly anybody had come to the special Mass in Res Sacra Miser, and that organized pastoral care for nurses had remained largely a strategic plan of the Polish Episcopate. Father Jerzy was the first of their chaplains to consider this state of affairs as his personal tragedy. But the nurses promised to help him. Within a short time a group of people were not only attending Mass regularly, but also meeting frequently in Father Jerzy's room. Once again a group of close friends was formed.

When Father Jerzy was asked to organize the voluntary medical personnel for Pope John Paul II's first visit to Poland in June 1979, he could already count on the help of many medical people. The service he organized was so impressive that Father Jerzy was again put in charge of setting up a medical group during the Pope's second visit to Warsaw in June 1983 . . . and earlier during the funeral of Cardinal Wyszynski. By then he had an army of volunteers, consisting not only of his medical students and the nurses, but also of many doctors – since the spring of 1980 he had been celebrating a special Mass for doctors on every second Sunday of the month.

The greatest achievement of his pastoral work among all sections of the medical community was to inspire them with his loving concern for life. Father Jerzy was always in the forefront of the struggle to defend the right to live. This also and always included the right to life of every unborn child. In the medical community of Warsaw he started to build his dream: a national movement for the protection of the unborn child. In his sermons, during lectures and retreats, he often recalled the vows taken by the whole nation in 1982 at Jasna Gora in Czestochowa – the spiritual capital of Poland. The entire Catholic population then vowed to defend every life, every unborn baby, and to die rather than harm a defenceless human being; they vowed to view the gift of life as the greatest treasure given to man by God, as the greatest treasure of the nation. Father Jerzy constantly reminded doctors of their Hippocratic oath: to save and not to kill. He saw abortion as a violation of the natural, universally binding law, as well as the breaking of God's fifth commandment: "Thou shalt not kill." It was he who persuaded many of them that every human law which violates God's law is in fact unlawful; one should not only not "have to" obey such laws, one *should* not obey them.

His work with the medical community was highly appreciated by his superiors, and on 15th October 1981 he was appointed chaplain to the medical communities throughout the diocese. A week before, on 6th October, at his own request he had also been appointed chaplain to the Warsaw home for retired medical personnel. Every Sunday after that he celebrated Mass there – first in the dining room and later in the new chapel, which he had furnished at his own expense.

In May of the year before, when it was apparent that his cumulative responsibilities were too much for him, he had been released from his duties at St Anna's church and moved back to the Zoloborz district, where he became a resident priest at the church of St Stanisław Kostka, a position usually reserved for retired priests. Thus when Father Jerzy was "settling down" to a quiet life as a medical chaplain he was still only thirty-two, and had seven years' pastoral ministry behind him, as well as two serious illnesses. His medical condition required constant treatment, and he was told that a quiet life free from strain, together with an appropriate diet, was essential to prevent any deterioration of his health. Paradoxically, however, Father Jerzy was about to embark on what was to become the most active part of his life. The time had come when his beliefs, his integrity and his adherence to the faith would indeed be put to the test.

In the summer of 1980 he spent a couple of weeks visiting his relatives in America, and returned to Poland on 30th July, just in time to witness and participate in one of the greatest phenomena of modern times – the creation of

Solidarity and the peaceful national revolution carried out under the banner of the Cross. According to those who had known him since childhood, he was never interested in the struggle against the political system, although like the majority of Polish people he saw the system as alien and as being kept in power only by Soviet arms. He was never actively involved in the dissident movement which had snowballed since 1976. That year the workers of Ursus, Płock and Radom had staged a strike in protest against the drastic increases in food prices. The local Party head-quarters in Radom were burnt down by angry workers, and there were clashes between the civilian crowds and the police. The revolt was soon crushed by the security police. Many workers were arrested, beaten up and even tortured. Many received long prison sentences, or lost their jobs with no hope of getting other employment.

It was then that a group of Warsaw intellectuals set up the Workers' Defence Committee (KOR). It collected money for imprisoned workers' families, provided the accused with legal aid, and publicized their plight in a special bulletin. Since then a powerful dissident movement had grown up despite police harassment. It concentrated on clandestine publishing, on filling the gaps in state education by means of lectures and discussion groups, and on organizing public demonstrations. All the opposition groups, however different their political programmes, agreed with certain principles the Church had been preaching for years. The process of social disintegration, essential for the existence of the communist system, could only be resisted through a moral revival. Through his pastoral work Father Jerzy was of course involved in this moral dimension of dissent, as were the other twenty thousand Polish priests and bishops, by preaching the Christian vision of man.

It was in the summer of 1980, at the time of the Polish "Revolution", that the story of Father Jerzy's mission among the workers began. In August the whole of Poland had its gaze fixed on the Lenin shipyard at Gdansk, where the inter-factory committee, led by Lech Wałesa, was for the first time in Poland's post-war history confronting representatives of the Polish communist authorities at the negotiating table. This was not a settlement between the coastal workers and the government – a new and more just social accord was being sought for the whole nation. If the authorities had agreed to come to the negotiating table, it was not because their hearts had suddenly been transformed or that they could no longer bring themselves – as had happened in Poznan in 1956 and in Gdansk in 1970 – to crush the workers' protests with truncheons and bullets. No, they came to Gdansk because they knew that this time they were confronting not just the workers of one region or even one social class; they were confronting the entire Polish nation. The nation as a whole was challenging the legitimacy of the government and its aptitude to lead the country. At that time the Leninist dogma of "political compromise, zig-zags, manoeuvres of conciliation and retreat" depending on "the advance or decline of the Revolution" came in very useful. In the summer of 1980 the communist revolution was not in decline – it was fighting for its very survival. An agreement between the workers and the government was reached, but for the authorities it was no more than a tactical manoeuvre, allowing them time to prepare a counter-attack. This came on 13th December 1981, only sixteen months after the creation of Solidarity, with the imposition of martial law.

In August 1980 almost all of Poland's industrial plants staged strikes in support of the Gdansk shipyard. A sympathy strike was also organized in the Warsaw steel plant. As in all the other big factories, the workers tried to find a priest who would celebrate Sunday Mass for them. A delegation of five workers from the steel plant arrived at the residence of Cardinal Wyszynski, claiming that most of the striking workers were practising Catholics and that they would like to participate in a Sunday Mass. The Cardinal told his chaplain, Father Bolesław Piasecki, "Find a priest." Father Piasecki went with the steel men to the Zoliborz parish of St Stanisław Kostka and bumped into Father Jerzy Popiełuszko, who listened to their problem and agreed at once to celebrate Mass for them. He swiftly went to ask his superior, Father Teofil Bogucki, for formal permission. Nobody at the steel plant can now remember precisely when or how Father Jerzy arrived there, though they all remember that first Mass he celebrated for the striking workers. It was a unique experience for Father Jerzy, who later described it in two of his interviews: "The memory of that workers' Mass at the Warsaw steel plant will stay with me until I die. I went there jittering. This situation was absolutely new. What would I find there? How would the workers receive me? Would there be a place suitable for celebrating the Mass? Who would do the readings? Who would sing the hymns? All these questions which today sound naïve then troubled my heart. And then at the gate I first began to feel astonished. The crowds of people – smiling and crying at the same time, and clapping. At first I thought that there was someone important right behind me. But they were clapping me – the first priest in the history of this plant to enter at the main gate. It then crossed my mind – that this applause was for the Church, which for the last thirty years had constantly knocked at the gates of the industrial plants. My earlier fears proved to be unfounded – everything was prepared for the Mass; the altar right in the middle of the factory square and the Cross, which later was placed at the main gate. It survived many hard days and still stands there, always surrounded by fresh flowers. There was even an improvised confessional. There were people to do the readings. It was worth hearing those men's voices, which so often used words you would certainly not near in a drawing room, but which now were solemnly reading out those holy texts. And then came the thunderlike response, 'Thanks be to God' – spoken by thousands. I also found that they could sing much better than people did in Church."' . . . "It was something extraordinary and made a great impression on me. It was there that the bond between us was born. I shared their anxiety. I heard the confessions of people who, tired beyond endurance, knelt on the pavement. Those people understood that their strength lay in God, in the unity within the Church."[2]

He remained with them day and night, celebrating Mass, hearing confessions, talking to them and upholding the spirit of hope. At this time a great depth of respect grew up between him and the workers. After the strike the workers offered Father Jerzy a job as their chaplain, which he gladly accepted. With the bishop's permission and the blessing of Father Teofil Bogucki, a generous man with a great heart, St Stanisław Kostka church became the official "parish" church for the Warsaw steel works. Even at this stage, it was known as a patriotic church, and carried a huge banner over its main entrance with the slogan "Bog i ojczyzna" (God and Our Country). Its walls bear many plaques commemorating heroic struggles from the nation's past.

Only a few months after its victory, black clouds started to gather over Solidarity. First the militia beat up local Solidarity leaders in Bydgoszcz, then came other provocations and food shortages, for which Solidarity alone was officially blamed. In a quiet unofficial amnesty, a large number of criminals were released from prisons nationwide, and all of a sudden the streets of Polish towns became as dangerous as those of New York. It was not only the Polish state-owned mass media but ordinary citizens who were talking more and more about the lack of law and order in the country and therefore the need to restore it. Then came the strike at a college for firemen in Warsaw. Father Jerzy, together with Seweryn Jaworski, vice-chairman of the regional branch of Solidarity, remained with the strikers. As he had during the strike at the Warsaw steel plant and then at the Medical Academy, he calmed down the hot-heads and brought spiritual and moral help. He also served as a messenger between the Primate of Poland and those on strike. For the first time his slender figure came in useful. He could get inside the college using back doors and small cellar windows. Right until the very end, the guards standing outside could not make out just how Father Jerzy was able to come and go almost as he pleased.

After breaking the strike in the college by force, the Polish authorities felt ready to "restore internal order". On 13th December 1981 martial law was declared, and thousands of Solidarity members and supporters were arrested and detained in internment camps. Father Jerzy kept up his close contacts with the workers. He believed that this was his duty as a priest: "The work of a priest is in a way an extension of the work of Christ. A priest is taken from the people and ordained for the people in order to serve them. So the duty of a priest is to be always with the people in both good and bad times. The duty of a priest is to be with the people when they need him most, when they are wronged, degraded and maltreated. For there is always suffering and pain where basic human rights are not respected, where there is no freedom of speech or opinion, where people are imprisoned for their convictions. And there are many such people in our country, especially since that December night in 1981. I felt that perhaps it was then that they needed me most, in those difficult times, praying for them in their prison cells, in the courtrooms where I went to hear their trials."[3]

Father Jerzy was the only priest who attended the trials regularly; he thought that his presence in court was natural and necessary. The people for whose spiritual life Father Jerzy felt responsible were on trial. He usually attended the trials together with the workers' families, and sat with them right at the front of the courtroom, embarrassing the judges. Here, for Father Jerzy, one thing was important: in seeing him the prisoners would know that their families were not without a friend, that they were cared for. The imprisoned and interned workers told him in their letters that they knew he was praying for them and how grateful they were for it, as it kept their spirits up. In court Father Jerzy formed many new friendships with people who had never heard of him before, but who nevertheless quickly learned to love and respect him. Among them was Professor Klemens Szaniawski: "I belong to the circle of Father Jerzy's friends, even though we are divided by age – twenty years, and in our times twenty years means a whole epoch. However, there are extraordinary circumstances which bring people with the same hierarchy of values together. There are also extraordinary people for whom the barriers of their experience of life, like any other barrier, do not matter. Father Jerzy was such a person. That is why I always think of him as someone very close."

After 13th December 1981 Father Jerzy added another to his many duties – that of comforting the families of the interned, and organizing material help for them as well as for their imprisoned relatives. He took care of families whose fathers had been thrown out of a job, of families with many children – in fact of anybody who in his judgement needed help. He seemed to know the needs of every family he temporarily took charge of. Whenever he came to the diocesan charitable centre, established at the beginning of martial law, he would recite from memory a long list of people and the exact items they needed: a jumper for this one, a pair of trousers size . . . for the other, milk for someone's baby. According to his parishioners, he never made a mistake or forgot about anybody. The wife of a steel worker recalls how once she told him in passing that she just could not make ends meet: her husband had lost his job because of his involvement in Solidarity's activities and the only work he could find after a lengthy search did not pay enough to keep them above the poverty line. Father Jerzy casually asked her about the difference in pay. She told him and after that, every month, Father Jerzy would arrive at their flat with "the difference".

In organizing material aid Father Jerzy relied on the help of people of goodwill both at home and abroad. In Warsaw he drew the attention of those who were better off to the needs of others, and encouraged industrial plants and institutions to take care of those families which were most in need of help. Relief supplies from abroad began to arrive in Poland. On the basis of personal contacts and friendships, Father Jerzy was recommended by people in Warsaw as a competent and energetic priest, and as a result some of the first Western relief transports arrived at St Stanisław Kostka Church. When the Church's system of charitable centres was set up, St Stanisław Kostka was chosen as Warsaw's first medical charitable centre, where foreign medicines could be obtained, and Father Jerzy was placed in charge of it. Sometimes people's generosity surpassed the modest storage space in the cellar and even Father Jerzy's efficient distribution, so that on at least one occasion there was no free space left but the church itself. Father Jerzy went to the parish priest, Father Teofil Bogucki, and obtained his permission to store the delivery in the church, with strict orders that it should be removed by the next Sunday. Each medical transport also brought clothing and food, for which Father Jerzy was always grateful. Soon an informal charitable centre was created at St Stanisław Kostka. Parcels, clothes and food were stored in the attic and also in Father Jerzy's room, as he tried to distribute all the gifts straightaway.

At the parish house where he lived he occupied just one room, divided by an old-fashioned bookcase into a sitting room and a bedroom. Next to that room was a tiny boxroom which contained the kitchen and lavatory. This strange arrangement always shocked newcomers to his quarters, but it didn't worry Father Jerzy. Even before it became a "store-house" his room was always untidy. Somehow he could never find the time for such apparent trivialities as tidying his room or hanging up his cassock properly. He would leave his scarf on the floor, and forget even to wash up his used cups and saucers – he would wash up only if he needed crockery in order to force a cup of tea on some tired guest! Children's clothes, shoes, various other items of clothing and food parcels were lying everywhere.

His day would begin at dawn. If he had visitors, after

celebrating an early Mass, he would have breakfast with them and with any other priest working in the parish. The latest "news" from the town was exchanged. Father Jerzy would, for example, tell the story of a brave granny who, hearing the police arriving to search her son's flat, quickly hid the Solidarity leaflets in a saucepan and put it in the oven. Then calm and composed she proceeded to assist the police in their vain attempt to find any incriminating material. Usually Father Jerzy had no time for breakfast, or indeed for any proper meal. Some of his closest friends told him on occasions that he represented a new human species – one that lives on air alone. There always seemed to be something more important to do than eat. From dawn to dusk Father Jerzy would be rushing around distributing medicine, delivering parcels or just conveying a comforting word. On the night of 13th–14th December 1982, when a bomb was thrown into his apartment in the early hours of the morning, he had just finished preparing Christmas parcels for the children in a nearby hospital. The Ministry of Health claimed it was short of money, so Father Jerzy felt it was his duty to help.

He was always working against the clock. On popping into his room for "a quiet moment alone" he usually found a crowd of people waiting for him. After the initial surprise, he would usually transform himself into the good host and run into his tiny kitchen to check whether he could offer them a cup of tea. Sometimes he could only stop for a few moments, with just enough time to put on his cassock and thank his friends for helping him button it up – he should already have been hearing confessions in the church ten minutes earlier!

Once he rushed into his room and informed all those present that some one hundred and sixty workers had been sacked that morning – he had to go immediately to make a list of them. He took some cans of food "just in case they need any", and rushed out.

There was a constant flow of people in Jerzy's room, "People come – they know that my home is open to them from morning till night." "Every day many people came who did not necessarily want material help. They wanted to talk, they wanted someone to share their sorrows and tears with them, to share their troubles. And the fact that I understood them and listened to them, that sometimes I had tears in my eyes, that I sympathized with their situation, their troubles and worries, often meant more to them than any material help."[4] At times Father Jerzy would bless the fact that there was a curfew, as this meant that he could have his room to himself. However, even with the curfew he still did not get enough rest as he spent many of his nights working. Only when he was absolutely exhausted would he go to a friend's house for a short nap. In his busy life the only relaxation he had, as he himself once said, was just before he went to bed: "I am on my knees before God, with no one else in sight."

Most of the people who drove the relief transports to Poland and met Father Jerzy remember him as someone constantly busy, always doing several things at the same time. During their (usually brief) encounters they were all impressed by his attitude towards them and the goods they had brought. Father Jerzy never asked what was inside the lorries. On their arrival he would immediately rush off to organize washing facilities and food for the drivers, often making sandwiches himself, as well as arranging their accommodation for the night. He would even make sure that the family they were placed with could speak their language. He would take the drivers to their lodgings himself, hastily returning to St Stanisław Kostka before the curfew. If the lorries arrived too late at night the drivers would sleep on the benches in the hall just outside Father Jerzy's room, or they would spend the whole night talking to him. He would never accept their offers to help unload the lorries – this was done by the army of volunteers which he seemed able to call up at a moment's notice. Father Jerzy certainly won the hearts of at least the British drivers in this way. For the majority of them these trips to Poland were only "a part of their job". Many were not even believers. There was, however, not a single driver who would not have given his or her right arm for Father Jerzy. "Father George", as they called him, was always the person to whom they wanted to deliver their load. Whatever Father George decided, they would obey to the letter.

What was it about him that moved the drivers so much? Was it his obvious example of hard work, his gratitude, his concern for their comfort, or maybe his sense of humour and the limitless number of badges and religious pictures – especially his favourite one of the Black Madonna – which he would offer them? One December a lorry from England arrived in Warsaw just in time for St Nicholas' Day (6th December) – a day which all Poles celebrate by exchanging gifts. A spontaneous St Nicholas party was organized in Father Jerzy's room and small presents were waiting for all those arriving at the party, including the drivers, who were quite taken aback by this gesture. Suddenly one of the drivers took off the heavy gold cross and chain he was wearing and handed it to Father Jerzy. He explained that, as an atheist, he had bought it as an investment during a holiday in Turkey, but now all of a sudden he wanted Father Jerzy to wear it. Father Jerzy treasured the gesture more than the cross, and after that party he always wore it – even on the day when he was kidnapped. (However, when Father Jerzy's body was found in the reservoir, the cross had gone.) Another English driver that night, who had also not thought of bringing a gift with him, took out his electronic lighter and shyly handed it to Father Jerzy, who was as happy with it as a child with a new toy. He would not allow anybody to touch it but endlessly offered cigarettes to everyone just so that he could use his lighter again. Everybody who came to see Father Jerzy that evening had to admire his new toy. Brought up in a tough rural environment, he always had a childlike attitude to all sophisticated twentieth-century gadgets. A bishop recalls how he met Father Jerzy on his return from America, when he was driving an impressive

American car. "Jerzy," the Bishop shook his head, "where did you get such a car?" Father Jerzy explained that it was a gift from his American aunt. "But none of the Polish bishops has got such a car", said the Bishop, disapproving of its expensive, ostentatious looks. "You should sell the car and buy something more modest – more suitable for a priest." Father Jerzy always listened to fair criticism and took the Bishop's advice.

What he really treasured most were the special souvenirs he had received from various people after 13th December 1981 in recognition of his pastoral work. These were all displayed in his room. For example, there was a replica of the Gdansk monument erected in 1980, which was given to him by the dockers. There was a cross with a red and white ribbon (the national colours of Poland) and the inscription "We shall come back", sculptured for him by the workers of Nowa Huta; there was a beautiful tapestry made by an anonymous admirer; a silver badge given to only a handful of people most involved in the strike at the Warsaw Steel Works and many, many others. Probably the most treasured item was a rosary given to him by the Polish Pope, John Paul II, as a token of his esteem and admiration.

Most of the meetings Father Jerzy had with his foreign visitors were chaotic, as he rarely had time to sit down and talk at length; but on occasions, when there was no business to attend to or more probably when it was too late to go out, he would sit down to have a cup of tea, and a conversation would start up. During one such meeting, when Father Jerzy was so tired that he was supporting his head with his hands, one of his foreign visitors noticed a number of holes in his shabby jumper. She turned to a Polish friend of his in reproach: "Can't you find a decent jumper for your priest?" The latter sighed and explained, "I had to give up. Whenever I gave him something he would always manage to meet someone with a greater need and give it to him." Father Jerzy examined his elbow and remarked with surprise, "Oh, yes! You are right. There are holes." He hadn't even noticed. Although he parted easily with anything of his own, it was a major task to persuade him to accept something personally. He always wore the most tattered shoes – even though in every delivery there was a pair of shoes brought especially for him. Father Jerzy always managed to find them too small or too big, and he "had to" give them away. He would accept a new pair only when his old shoes had died a natural death. Then strangely enough, the size did not seem to matter! A friend visiting him once in Warsaw noticed that Father Jerzy had developed a peculiar tendency to trip over everything. The explanation was simple: when the time had come to choose a new pair of shoes the first pair he came upon were sandals two sizes too big. He could not understand the fuss his friend had made. After all, he suggested, he could cut off a piece to make them smaller. In the end he solemnly promised to wear the proper sized sandals which she would send him. Two months later she received a short message from Warsaw: "The sandals are already walking." Father Jerzy always kept his promise.

At the beginning of martial law, when food shortages were most severe, one of the transport lorries had also brought him a food parcel. The drivers had heard of Father Jerzy's hospitality and did not want to burden him by their visit. He refused to accept it so they just put the parcel on the floor in the middle of the room. Half an hour later someone came to see Father Jerzy, who opened the parcel and gave the visitor a tin of food. This was repeated until the entire contents of the parcel had disappeared – all before the despairing gaze of the drivers. The same thing happened to a box of oranges and apples brought to him as a Christmas gift. Every person who, for any reason, came to see him at that time, was given a piece of fruit on their arrival. In distributing material aid Father Jerzy always followed the same reasoning: it was better to give to nine unworthy men than to refuse one who really needed help.

Though most of his encounters with foreign guests were brief, he formed many instant but lasting friendships.

Often he also became their spiritual counsellor and helped them to solve various personal problems. Father Jerzy was a loyal friend and one with imagination. He once asked a friend what he should get him for Christmas: "Some Polish Christmas decorations" was the reply. Later that day Father Jerzy bought a box of beautiful Christmas glass balls with a red and white eagle painted on them (the Polish national emblem). Another friend who was leaving Poland decided, after long hesitation, not to take any of the Solidarity badges or leaflets he had been given for fear of being stopped at the customs post and subsequently not being allowed back into Poland again. He rang Father Jerzy from the airport; to his disappointment the priest was not at home, although by rights he should have been, as he had just finished celebrating Mass. The visitor had to go on and board the plane. As he left the airport building he suddenly heard a familiar voice calling his name from the terrace above. He looked up – there was Father Jerzy waving at him and asking him to throw something on the ground. He threw down his passport and a moment later a tiny Solidarity badge, no larger than a quarter of a finger nail, landed on top of it. To be at the airport with this gift meant that Father Jerzy had had to swap Masses with another priest. The foreign visitor waved a thank you, pinned on the Solidarity badge and proudly entered the plane.

By the end of 1982, Father Jerzy's meetings with foreigners were becoming rare. His charitable work was being slowly overtaken by work of another kind, although of course he still remained very concerned for the material needs of "his people" and active in helping them; he organized various excursions and, in the summer of 1984, even managed to organize a summer holiday for needy families in Oswiecim (Auschwitz). On his initiative special educational courses for the workers were organized at the parish church on Catholic social thought, courses which quickly acquired the name of "The Workers' University". Large numbers of workers regularly attended these lectures, which pleased Father Jerzy very much. He dreamt of a whole network of similar "universities" organized on a national scale and modelled on the Christian workers' universities set up in Włocławek by Cardinal Stefan Wyszynski before the Second World War. Father Jerzy was convinced that these courses were essential in filling the gaps left by the state educational system. "Remember, only knowledgeable people can propose an alternative political system to the totalitarian one in the future", he would say to the "students".

1 Interview published in *Ład Bozy*, a Catholic bi-weekly, No. 9, 1983.
2 Unpublished interview.
3 Unpublished interview.
4 Unpublished interview.

# 4

# Towards Solidarity of Hearts

"You must be strong with the strength of faith,
You must be strong with the strength of hope,
You must be strong with the strength of love,
Love which will endure everything.
A Nation, as a community of people, is called to victory,
   to victory by
The power of hope and love, to victory through the
   power of truth, freedom and justice."

(Pope John Paul II, Krakow, 1983)

*

"Always remain with the people. As their shepherds, try
to defend our country, our common responsibility and
never forget that you are Poles."

(Archbishop Antoni Fijałkowski, 1861 – to Polish priests)

*

"We are called to the truth. We are called to witness to the
truth with our whole lives. 'You will know the truth and the
truth will make you free' (John 8:32). Let us be faithful to
the truth."

(Father Jerzy Popiełuszko, October 1982)

*

Martial law had been declared in December 1981. It was
on the night of 13th December, as thousands of Solidarity
members and supporters were arrested, that Father Jerzy
knew that spiritual aid was the most important help a priest
could give – above everything else. Over and above
material comfort he wanted to give the victims his prayers,
and to place their sufferings before God. It was then, in the
courtroomswhere he went to hear the trials of the Warsaw

43

steel men, that Father Jerzy had the idea of holding special Masses for all those who were imprisoned, and for their families. During the Mass – one of the most perfect forms of prayer that the people of God can offer the Father of all people and nations – their sufferings could also be offered to Christ so that God might transform them into His blessings. "We must realize that we must not waste this enormous burden of the nation's sufferings but should offer it to God in humble and trustful prayer. Too much blood, pain, tears and misery have been placed at Christ's feet that they cannot fail to return from God as a gift of true freedom, justice and love" (Father Jerzy, Mass for the Country, November 1983).

In January 1982 a Mass was organized as part of the series of Masses for the Country (MFC) which were already being celebrated, even before martial law, in St Stanisław Kostka Church. On this occasion, Father Jerzy preached the first of the "patriotic sermons" that were to bring him the esteem and admiration of many but which were also to lead to his martyrdom. Just one month after the introduction of martial law, when the death penalty threatened anyone making an "anti-state pronouncement", Father Jerzy Popiełuszko limited his sermon to one crucial sentence: "Because freedom of speech has been taken away from us by the introduction of martial law, let us, whilst listening to the voice of our heart and conscience, think of those brothers and sisters who have been deprived of their freedom." Three minutes of silence followed. A month later he celebrated a similar Mass, and after April 1982 Masses for those suffering under martial law were to become a regular feature in his parish life.

The seven o'clock Mass on the last Sunday evening of each month attracted an ever increasing number of people, and was more and more widely referred to as the "Mass for the Country". People from all walks of life participated in these Masses: workers and intellectuals, actors and university professors, famous and respected Poles as well as anonymous ones, both young and old, Warsovians and people from all corners of Poland. The church became too small to accommodate the tens of thousands who were coming, so they would fill the large square outside, regardless of the weather. Masses for the Country were celebrated in many churches throughout Poland, so what was so special about this Mass? During the Mass celebrated by Father Popiełuszko the cream of Poland's acting profession recited works by the country's best poets and thinkers, carefully selected by Father Jerzy himself. In this way people were reminded of the long history of Poland's sufferings, but also of their forefathers' determination never to relinquish responsibility for the country's well-being. They were reminded that it was the faith that had given their forefathers courage and which had never let them give up hope for a free and Christian Poland. Those present felt that the atmosphere during the Masses celebrated by Father Jerzy was quite unique, though difficult to describe. It embraced "solemnity and community", there was a sense of unity with others and at the same time a feeling that one was just a particle of something which surpassed everything. Some described the Masses as a kind of mediaeval mystery: the old liturgical texts seemed to have a hidden Polish meaning, and people realized how similar the fate of contemporary Poles was to that of the first Christians.

"If the Mass was so popular," Father Jerzy once said, "it was because it included all those who had suffered, those who had been wronged. People went away conscious of a great unity, a common goal, strengthened in the hope that good would conquer evil. They knew that they were not alone in their sorrows and their troubles, that there were thousands and thousands of Poles who thought like them."[1] People came to pour out their anguish in prayer, in spontaneous song and in the solidarity of silence before God – but also to hear Father Jerzy preach. His sermons expressed his desire to "include God in the difficult and painful problems of the country", and his conviction that in bearing witness to the truth the Church could not be neutral in the face of injustice and human suffering, but must become the first defender of the oppressed.

"It is not only the hierarchy," Father Jerzy believed, "but the millions of believers who in the broadest sense embody the Church. So when people suffer and are persecuted the Church also feels the pain. The mission of the Church is to be with the people and to share in their joys and sorrows." As a modern disciple of Christ, Father Jerzy understood his vocation very clearly: "To serve God is to seek a way to human hearts. To serve God is to speak about evil as a sickness which should be brought to light so that it can be cured. To serve God is to condemn evil in all its manifestations" (MFC, March 1983).

Father Jerzy Popiełuszko spent a long time preparing each of his sermons. He read widely, but more importantly he listened to people. Wherever he went he would always carry a small notebook with him to jot down people's personal experiences, a striking sentence or even a word. "When I think something is true, I say it in my sermon because I feel that it should be known to others, so that we can all pray for it." He always read his sermons to working people to check whether they understood everything. "If a worker understands, so will a university professor", he used to say. When Father Jerzy spoke, a unique silence would descend upon the enormous congregation. As a gifted orator he expressed fearlessly the thoughts that others were unable or afraid to utter. His words were powerful but did not incite anyone to violence – quite the contrary. His treatment of the issues of the day was courageous and direct. He spoke of "a nation terrorized by military forces", of families shattered by martial law, "of people detained and brought to trial, their only guilt being their determination to remain faithful to the ideals of Solidarity" (MFC, April 1982). He described "attempts to send healthy internees to mental institutions" (MFC, March 1983), "the beatings and ill-treatment of the many prisoners in the internment camps scattered throughout Poland", and the "many crimes of Cain", such as the crime committed against a young man of nineteen, Grzegorz Przemyk, by members of the security police in May 1983. Father Jerzy mentioned "people losing their jobs merely because they did not want to give up their membership of Solidarity", and "teachers sacked from their jobs because they wanted to pass on to young people a true love of their country". He also spoke of the "mass media being used to slander those respected by society", of "tragedies suffered by children whose parents have been imprisoned or have had to go into hiding, the irreversible psychological shock suffered by children faced with brutal evil and hatred" (MFC, June 1982). "Whose conscience will be burdened by the orphans of martial law? In our prayers we turn to you, Lord Jesus, whose heart was pierced by the spear of malefactors, whose heart suffered so much. You were also once a child and though you had a Heavenly Father, God gave you St Joseph who performed the duties of an earthly father. As a child you suffered when you were forced to run away from your country because of Herod's hired assassins. So you understand the pain of children, whose parents have to live in hiding like criminals even though they are not, the pain of children whose parents are still in the internment camps and prisons" (MFC, June 1982). Father Jerzy Popiełuszko did not hesitate to compare the suffering of Poland with the suffering of Christ on Calvary: "The trial of Christ is still going on. Christ is being tried in the person of His brothers. Only their names and faces, the dates and places of their birth have changed. The methods change but the trial of Christ still goes on. All who cause pain and suffering to their brothers are fighting against what Christ died for on the Cross. All those who try to build on lies, deceit and half-truths, who degrade human dignity, the dignity of God's children, the dignity valued so much by God Himself, are participating in that fight. What a likeness there is today between Christ bleeding on the Cross and our unfortunate country! Like Christ on the Cross our country is bleeding from her wounds. Her sons are being deprived of honour and dignity, are humiliated and often downtrodden. Christ was killed on the Cross by His own countrymen, in His own country. Today our brothers are also being killed by their fellow countrymen. How many crosses we could name which our nation has to bear. Our greatest cross is the lack of respect for basic human rights . . . The late Primate, Cardinal Wyszynski, expressed this in his own words thus, 'The basis of all social order and the condition for order throughout the world, for peace in one's conscience, in families, in nations – is respect for basic human rights.' Where these rights to truth, freedom and justice are not respected there is not and cannot be peace. Firstly, these human rights have to be recognized and then we should start to build peace together. In our country human rights are not respected because thousands of people are still in camps and prisons. Many untrue words are being relayed by the mass media, but justice is not respected. It is the cross of our country that for years there has been a strange desire to deprive people of God – especially the young – and to inflict an ideology which has nothing to do with the thousand-year-old Christian tradition of our nation. 'How can anybody think' – I'm quoting the late Primate [Wyszynski] – 'that Poland, which for ten centuries has lived in the light of the Cross and the Gospel, would renounce Christ and abandon her own Christian culture, formed over centuries, implanted in the lives of individuals, families and the nation as a whole?' Planned atheization, the struggle against God and everything that is of God, is a struggle against human greatness and dignity. Man is great because he carries within himself the dignity of a child of God. Another cross is our lack of truth. Such is the nature of truth that it comes to light, however scrupulous and planned the attempts to hide it are . . . The cross is also the lack of freedom. Where there is no freedom, there is no love, no friendship between the members of the family, within the nation or between nations. It is not possible to love or form a relationship with someone by force. Modern man is more sensitive to love than force. Poles cannot be won by threats. And 'fortitude does not mean carrying a weapon', as the late Primate said, 'for fortitude comes from the heart, not from weapons.' Every one of us standing here today could name an endless number of crosses, which he or she has experienced personally or witnessed, especially during the last ten months, months of constant anxiety, ill-treatment and fear, months with an uncertain future" (MFC, September 1982).

Like some Old Testament prophet, Father Jerzy Popiełuszko did not hesitate to address the authorities directly: "The nation seeks unity and co-operation but it also demands a guarantee that it will not be misled again, and that its efforts will not go to waste. It seeks compromise without capitulation or renunciation of its ideals, its aspirations or its faith in a better and more worthy future" (MFC, March 1983).

He offered the authorities a long and detailed list of the factors preventing reconciliation: "The bitter humiliation and helplessness which many people suffer daily does not assist reconciliation. The trials of those who have been democratically elected as representatives of the workers do not assist reconciliation. Shattered families do not assist reconciliation nor do children who long for their imprisoned parents, wives awaiting the return of their husbands, mothers awaiting their sons and daughters. Rounding up people returning home peacefully from church services does not assist reconciliation, nor do demonstrations of force in the street, near the churches where people pray . . . Reconciliation is not served by documents which state that a Solidarity activist who undertakes to form a new union at his place of work will have his salary doubled, but that if he wants to remain faithful to his conscience he will be demoted and transferred to a different factory on the other side of Warsaw . . . All these wrongs committed against the people must be put right and we should sit down at a table intending to find the way out together. The common goal should be reconciliation – the well-being of the country and respect for human dignity. Our hands should be stretched out towards reconciliation in the spirit of love, but also in the spirit of justice, for as the Holy Father said five years ago, 'Love cannot exist without justice, love outgrows justice but at the same time it finds reaffirmation in justice'" (MFC, March 1983).

"And justice means acknowledgement of the rights due to each individual; fair pay for honest work, with no fear of dismissal or demotion for holding personal views concerning the good of the nation. Justice is the equality of all citizens before the law. Every court must be free and impartial . . . Justice means being able to answer the slanders thrown at Lech Wałesa by the Polish mass media in the last few weeks. Justice means pluralism for trade unions, and for creative groups which were promised under martial law. Justice would allow young people to form their personality according to models chosen by themselves and not those officially imposed on them. Justice means an amnesty involving total acquittal for the 'crimes' committed under the martial law decree. It means rectifying all wrongs, especially moral wrongs. It means a public agreement with a guarantee that people will not be cheated again, that the present time – when we are building up our country – will not turn out once more to be a period of mistakes and deviations, that the hard work of the nation will not be wasted" (MFC, August 1983).

Meditating on current problems, Father Jerzy Popiełuszko always touched upon the wider issues involved such as the nature of authority and government, justice and the fundamental human right to freedom, independence and dignity. He was convinced that the problems of Poland stemmed from the forceful exclusion of God from social and political life, and of Christian ethics from the process of governing.

"In his message for the Day of Peace . . . the Holy Father, John Paul II, stated: 'Government means service. The first love of the authorities should be for those whom they govern. And if this really were the case, if this basic Christian truth became part of real life, if the authorities behaved morally, if Christian ethics dominated the principles of the government, how different our lives would be. However, we have become witnesses to tyrannical states, where communication with the citizen takes the form of orders from the police'" (MFC, August 1982).

"These are the fundamental features of a lawful government:

1. The government must play the part of a servant towards the nation . . .
2. The government must always follow the truth and justice . . .
3. The government should create happiness for all, asking from each individual only what he or she can give, without any kind of coercion.

"Any government which has no means of implementing its policies other than the use of force is not a government but a blasphemous usurper, and the people are as defenceless as an unarmed man confronted by a highway robber. Even if this man were as innocent and as holy as Christ Himself, nothing could save him, neither his religion nor the law nor any moral norms. The cry of Abel only arouses the fury of his brother Cain. You cannot expect anything good from people who do not respect your dignity or freedom" (MFC, August 1982).

Father Jerzy frequently reminded his listeners that freedom was a gift to man from God, and that any violation of freedom, especially freedom of conscience, constituted opposition to God Himself. "The whole activity of Jesus Christ was aimed at making people realize that they were created for the freedom of the children of God. God created man in His image, so he is free; indeed, man can accept or reject his Creator, love would not exist if we were *forced* to love. Where then did all enslavement come from? Why are there prisons? There are invisible prisons, many of them. There are prisons in which people are born and die. There are prisons of system and structure. There are the prisons which not only confine the body but penetrate further, right into the human spirit – destroying inner freedom. Man has also built prisons of bricks and mortar, surrounded by barbed wire and high walls. And though these prisons are sometimes needed because the system of God's values has been destroyed by man, they should not be used to confine those who think and feel differently and seek the good of the country in alternative ways" (MFC, February 1983).

While condemning evil, Father Jerzy also spoke out against any thought of hatred or revenge, and pointed to the Cross of the Resurrection – "The sign of the victory of good over evil, life over death and love over hatred." During every Mass he prayed not only for those who had been wronged but also for those "who cause human suffering, anxiety and fear", for those "who violate human conscience", for "lawyers representing justice, who do not have the courage to oppose lies and falsehood", for those "who are in the service of injustice", that God would open their eyes and help them to see and accept the truth.

"Do not fight by means of violence. Violence is a sign of weakness. Whatever cannot win by influencing the heart tries to win by means of violence. The most splendid and lasting battles known to history are the battles of human thought. The most ignoble and the shortest are the battles of violence. An idea which needs weapons to survive, will die by itself. The idea which prevails merely through the use of violence is perverted. A living idea conquers by itself. It is followed by millions" (MFC, December 1982).

"Through Christ's death and resurrection the Cross – a symbol of disgrace – became a symbol of courage, virtue, help and brotherhood. In the sign of the Cross we embrace today all that is most beautiful and valuable in man. Through the Cross we go on to resurrection. There is no other way. And therefore the crosses of our country, our personal crosses and those of our families, must lead to victory, to resurrection, if we are united with Christ who conquered the Cross" (MFC, September 1982).

In Lent 1982 Father Jerzy had said: "Let this Holy Week

and Easter be a time of prayer for us – who raise up the cross of our sufferings, the cross of salvation. And for you, brothers, who hide 'paid for' hatred in your hearts, let it be a time of reflection, so that violence does not win, even though it can triumph for a time. We have the best proof of this in the Cross of Christ. Then there was also hatred of the truth. But violence and hatred were overcome by the love of Christ. Let us be strong through love, praying for our brothers who have been misled, without condemning anybody but condemning and unmasking evil. Let us pray in the words of Christ spoken from the Cross, 'Father, forgive them, for they know not what they do' (Luke 13:24). And give us, O Christ, an even greater awareness that love is stronger than violence and hatred" (MFC, March 1982).

With the loving concern of a follower of Christ he turned to the oppressors: "There is a man of God in every man. Look at yourself, brothers, to see whether you have not almost erased it. Regardless of your profession, you are a man, no less than a man . . . God will never abandon His children, even those who turn their backs on Him. And therefore everybody has a chance. Even if you lost everything, as humans understand it, if you lost your self-respect and sold yourself totally, you still have time. Brace yourself, stand up. Try to build on what is God's inside you. Try, for you have only one life" (MFC, January 1984).

A staunch supporter of Solidarity, Father Jerzy often referred to the Solidarity period as "the awakening of the nation's conscience"; a patriotic struggle to reinstate human dignity; a spontaneous expression of national identity and the desire of working men to be answerable to their own country, their own people and themselves. Father Jerzy recalled the origins of Solidarity through the words of the late leader of the Polish Church, Cardinal Stefan Wyszynski: "Over the last forty years, working people have fallen victim to many deceptions and restrictions. Workers and society as a whole have experienced violation of basic human rights – restriction of freedom of thought, speech and outlook, of freedom of worship and freedom to educate the young in a religious manner. The dependent work force comprised a special model of employees trained to silence and efficient work. When this oppression had exhausted everybody sufficiently, a device for freedom emerged. Solidarity came into being" (MFC, January 1983).

"The 'Solidarity' born in August 1980 was not only the trade union of that name, which was formed a few months later, but the united desire of the whole nation for truth, justice and freedom. That this was a national solidarity is proved by the fact that martial law was directed against the whole nation and not only against the trade union" (MFC, August 1984).

"Solidarity is the unity of hearts, minds and hands, rooted in ideals which are capable of changing the world for the better. It is the hope of millions of Poles. The more that hope is united with the source of all hope – God – the stronger it becomes. As the Pope said after his return from Africa – Solidarity is the synonym for unity and community. This word has been given a deep meaning by the Poles of the eighties. It is a loud call to respect human rights, to take notice of your neighbour and his problems. It means concern for the imprisoned, demands for their release, and care for their families. It means brotherly concern for everybody who is persecuted and discriminated against for their beliefs, which we all share. It is a duty to fight evil and its actions. It means that we should tell young people about many historical events which are never mentioned in our country. Solidarity is a constant concern for our country, upholding its internal freedom even in conditions of enslavement. It means that we must overcome paralysing fear, upholding our dignity as children of God and courageously bearing witness to what we believe, what we hold in our hearts" (MFC, August 1983).

After martial law had been imposed, Father Jerzy rejected outright all official claims that Solidarity had been destroyed. "Let no one say that Solidarity has lost. It is walking towards victory, walking slowly, but merging ever more strongly with the nation. It [Solidarity] still has to suffer a great deal to purify itself like gold in a melting pot, but August 1980 showed the correct road to take for a new generation of people living in the love of truth, courage and brotherly love" (MFC, November 1983).

"That which is in the heart, which is deep within a man, cannot be destroyed by any decrees or bans. I think we could call to mind here the story told of one of the poor African states, where the country's leader forbade its citizens to use the word 'hunger' under threat of severe penalties, and then announced to the world that the problem of hunger had been solved in his country. In our country the same problem exists and will go on existing, for Solidarity hopes to satisfy the hunger of the human heart, the hunger for love, justice and truth. This word 'Solidarity' should not be treated with contempt and assigned to the allegedly disgraceful past. It is a word of which the whole world speaks with reverence, which the Holy Father called praiseworthy and which [through its leader, Lech Wałesa] was given the highest award – the Nobel Peace Prize. The hopes of August 1980 still live" (MFC, August 1984).

"Solidarity is like a gigantic tree, which in spite of the fact that its roots are continuously being cut off, keeps putting out new ones . . . and it stays in the soil of our country . . . Solidarity is still the hope of many millions of people, united in prayer with God, and nobody can kill that hope" (MFC, August 1983).

"A nation with a thousand years of Christian tradition behind it will always seek full freedom. The yearning for freedom cannot be stopped by violence, as violence is the weapon of those who do not possess the truth. Man can be crushed by violence but not enslaved. Poles who love God and their country will rise again after any humiliation, for they have knelt only before God" (MFC, January 1983).

Pointing to the Christian duty of fortitude, Father Jerzy

Popiełuszko offered a vision of liberation through non-violent psychological resistance in conditions where fear and repression are the norm: "A Christian fulfils his duties only when he is stalwart, when he professes his principles courageously, when he is neither ashamed of them nor renounces them because of fear or material needs. Woe betide a society whose citizens do not live by fortitude! They cease to be citizens and become more like slaves. It is fortitude which creates citizens, for only a courageous man is conscious of all his rights and duties. If a citizen lacks fortitude, he becomes a slave and causes immeasurable harm not only to himself but to his family, his country and the Church . . . Woe betide state authorities who want to govern citizens by threats and fear! Fortitude is an essential part of one's life as a citizen. That is why fortitude is, for a Christian, the most important duty after love" (MFC, April 1983).

"In order to remain spiritually free men, we must live in truth. To live in truth means to bear witness to it to the outside world at all times and in all situations. The truth is unchangeable. It cannot be destroyed by any decree or law. The source of our captivity lies in the fact that we allow lies to reign, that we do not denounce them, that we do not protest against their existence every day of our lives, that we do not confront lies with the truth but keep silent or pretend that we believe in the lies. Thus we live in a state of hypocrisy. Courageous witness to the truth leads directly to freedom. A man who bears witness to the truth can be free even though he might be in prison. If the majority of Poles set out on the way of truth today, if the majority had not forgotten a year ago what truth is, we would even now become more spiritually free as a nation. External freedom or political freedom would come too, sooner or later – as the consequence of this freedom of spirit and faithfulness to the truth . . . The essential thing in the process of liberating man and the nation is to overcome fear. Fear stems from threats. We fear suffering, we fear losing material good, we fear losing freedom or our work. And then we act contrary to our consciences, thus muzzling the truth. We can overcome fear only if we accept suffering in the name of a greater value. If the truth becomes for us a value worthy of suffering and risk, then we shall overcome fear – the direct reason for our enslavement. Christ told His followers: 'Be not afraid of them that kill the body, and after that have no more that they can do'" (Luke 12:4) (MFC, October 1982). "A nation dies when it lacks fortitude, when it deceives itself by saying that everything is well when it is not, when it is satisfied with only half-truths. Let this thought be with us every day, that if we demand the truth from others, then we ourselves must live by it. If we demand justice, we ourselves must be just towards the people who are close to us. If we demand courage and fortitude we ourselves must always be courageous" (MFC, May 1984).

"We must overcome fear, which paralyses and enslaves the thoughts and hearts of men. Here I want to repeat a sentence uttered by me many times from the pulpit: the only thing we should fear is the betrayal of Christ for a few silver pieces of meaningless peace" (MFC, August 1984).

Father Jerzy pointed to Christ as the example to follow: "God loved the world so much that He gave His only son, Jesus Christ, to the world. He did this to give people an example of perfect humanity . . . to show the people the simplest, though not the easiest, way of life which can lead us to the home of the Heavenly Father, whose children we all are. This 'childhood in God' gives us, though we are weak people, a task for life. A Christian must be the salt of the earth and the light of the world. A Christian must be a sign of contradiction in the world, contradicting all kinds of evil, violence, mendacity, enslavement, hypocrisy. A Christian must be the light showing the world that God is one, the Lord of Heaven and Earth, who is Love and Good; and that all other lords guided by hatred, force or lies are in the service of God's enemy – in the service of Satan. A Christian is one who all his life chooses between good and evil, lies and truth, love and hatred, God

57

and Satan. A Christian is a man who chooses between the road to eternal life and purely earthly perspectives. A Christian is a man who chooses between being a slave and being courageous and just. Today more than ever there is a need for our light to shine, so that through us, through our deeds, through our choices, people can see the Father who is in Heaven. As the children of God, we cannot be frightened slaves for Christ's Kingdom, as the Holy Father has said . . . It carries within itself the heritage of freedom . . . We must believe that we will live through all the hard times and will reach a brighter future, but on condition that we are guided by greatness of spirit, courage of thought and action, that we are guided by law and conscience, truth and justice, by the consciousness that God loved the world so much that He gave His Son as an example. We believe that we will live to see better times, when there will be more Christians, for whom in his prayer . . . the Holy Father thanked Our Lady of Jasna Gora in the following words: 'Thank you, O Mother, for all who remain faithful to their conscience, for all who may be themselves fighting their own weaknesses, giving strength to others.' I would like to thank you, Mother, for all who do not give in to evil but overcome evil through love. That type of victory, the victory of good over evil (with our participation) – nobody will be able to take away that victory over ourselves, over our own egoism, over our faint-heartedness and fear, and that type of victory is what I wish for you all and for myself" (17th June 1984).

The essence of Father Jerzy's vision of liberation lies in the concept of "Solidarity of Hearts" first offered to the Poles by Pope John Paul II, and here in Father Jerzy's own words:

"Do we remember our brothers and sisters who were sentenced under martial law for defending the dignity of the workers? They were sentenced because they tried to remain faithful to their ideals and dreams, shared openly by millions of others in 1980. How important it is for them, but also for us, to feel that the solidarity of hearts still exists, that their problems are ours. How important is the knowledge that their families are cared for materially and spiritually; the knowledge that every day we include the innocently imprisoned in our evening prayers, that we teach our children to pray for our country, for our ideals. Satan will strengthen his earthly kingdom in our country, unless we become stronger in God and His grace, unless we show care and love for those of our brothers who suffer innocently in prisons, and for their troubled families. There are places where the families of the imprisoned are cared for and respected. But there are also places where fear is stronger than moral duty. Remember what Christ said: 'In as much as ye have done it unto one of the least of these my brethren ye have done it unto me'" (Matthew 26:40).

After Father Jerzy's murder, the following extract from his sermons became the most widely quoted by the Polish people: "Let us put the truth, like a light, on a candlestick, let us make life in truth shine out, if we do not want our conscience to putrefy . . . Let us not sell our ideals for a mess of pottage. Let us not sell our ideals by selling our brothers. It depends on our concern for our innocently imprisoned brothers, on our life in truth, how soon that time comes when we shall share our daily bread again in solidarity and love. At this time, when we need so much strength to regain and uphold our freedom, let us pray to God to fill us with the power of His Spirit, to reawaken the spirit of true solidarity in our hearts" (MFC, February 1983).

1 Unpublished interview.

# 5

# Trials and Tribulations

Father Popiełuszko's vision of man held very little appeal for the Polish atheist authorities; they saw the services for Poland as "rallies hostile to the Polish state". Father Popiełuszko was accused of political activity and of inciting people to violence. The authorities were determined to prove their point, so the constant threat of provocation by the police was ever present. Before each Mass Father Jerzy's nerves were stretched near to their limit. He felt totally responsible for the safety of the people participating in the Masses. Every electricity point had to be guarded in case the public address system was switched off, and voluntary "orderlies" were dispersed among the congregation. To discourage the troublemakers who on a number of occasions had tried to turn the Mass into a political demonstration, the "orderlies" would put on their means of identification just before each Mass began, and the priest would announce from the altar which colour armband or type of badge was in use by the genuine volunteers that day. The people were also reminded that this was a meeting for prayer, and were asked not to display any banners or flags either inside or outside the church. After the Mass Father Popiełuszko would make a plea to the congregation: "I ask all the faithful not to listen to the provocateurs who are here among us and who try to call for a song or demonstration after the Mass. Let us agree that after the Mass only provocateurs will sing or shout slogans outside the church. By keeping calm and restraining ourselves we shall see just how many there are among us. Let us bear witness to our maturity. Let us force the provocateurs to go away empty-handed." He would also appeal to the provocateurs themselves, "And you brothers who were ordered to come here by others, if you want to serve the truth and keep your self-respect, let the faithful go home in peace."

To many of the participants at Mass, one moment above all others seemed to stay in their hearts and memories. It was when Father Jerzy, reciting the liturgical formula, "Let us offer each other a sign of peace", used to add in his own words, "and let us not be led by a feeling of hatred." For while the thousands of people repeated these words, often trying to overcome their inner resentment only with the utmost difficulty, a cordon of ZOMO (riot squad) police stood just a few yards away; they were armed with water cannon, ready and probably eager to move into action. The people would, however, leave the church and solemnly walk past this cordon of hatred, full of joy and forgiveness. "They were enriched by the purity of tone given to Father Jerzy by God Himself", as Andrzej Szczepkowski, a well-known Polish actor, put it during his speech at the priest's funeral.

The difference between politics and religion lies in the heart of man, and Father Jerzy knew that he was not a politician. He once explained his attitude: "What I do is not political. For me the pastoral dimension is the most important. I base my sermons on the teaching of Pope John Paul II and of the late Cardinal Wyszynski. My strategy is founded on the fight against hatred, for the dignity of human labour. My weapons are truth and love."

Pointing to his tiny room Father Jerzy once said to a visiting priest, "Here people kneel to reconcile themselves with God after many years, twenty, even forty. Sometimes whole families come together to confession. For a priest there can be no greater joy or reward. Many of them are people who first came to the 'Mass for the Country' out of curiosity or out of patriotic duty, and were led to Christ." A student told Father Jerzy once that on first attending Mass he felt as if he were at the theatre. The next time he sensed that he was in communion with the others present

– people experiencing the same feelings as he did. After that he spent the whole night in prayer. He embraced Father Popiełuszko and said, "Imagine, Father, I, who never said a prayer in my life, I sat at the table with my head in my hands and prayed the whole night." Two months later he came back again and told Father Jerzy that he had been to confession and communion at the shrine of Jasna Gora. "I could quote many similar cases", continued Father Jerzy. "Not so long ago I baptized a student who told me that during the strike at the Medical Academy he was jealous of us because we had the support of the Mass and thus had grounds for hope, while he felt suspended in a great emptiness. That made him think and search. I must say that never before had I seen a man so well prepared for baptism and life in the faith."[1]

Father Jerzy received hundreds of letters, which mostly described how the "Mass for the Country" had helped the writers not to lose hope, and to overcome the hatred which tended to swell up inside them against their will. There were also a few evil letters full of hatred and threats – naturally enough, anonymous.

At first the authorities tried to silence Father Popiełuszko through the Church. In 1982 two letters had been sent to the Warsaw Curia informing them of the "anti-state tone" of Father Jerzy's sermons. The letter dated 30th August 1982, which was signed by Adam Łopatka, the Minister for Religious Affairs, listed Father Jerzy's "crimes": ". . . Father Popiełuszko, without obtaining the necessary permits, had made use of the public address system of the surroundings of the church, thus assembling a crowd of about five thousand people who blocked the traffic in the streets. Father Popiełuszko had permitted the active participation of certain lay people in the service, one of whom prayed for the victims of martial law. During the service there was a collection for those 'wronged by martial law'. Moreover, Father Popiełuszko's attitude, as well as the atmosphere that he himself created, resulted in the transformation of a religious gathering into a political

The seminarian

Army service

**Above** With Father Henryk Jankowski and Lech Wałesa

**Right** In prayer: a mass for the country

**Above opposite** Father Teofil Bogucki

**Below opposite** May 1983: Father Jerzy comforts the mother of Grzegorz Przemyk, killed by security police

31st October 1984: Father Jerzy's parents at St Stanisław Kostka Church

Warsaw steel workers place a replica of the Solidarity banner in the grave of Father Jerzy

demonstration, risking a breakdown of law and order in the capital . . . The above mentioned behaviour . . . contributes towards increasing alarm among the public and excites rowdy individuals." Mr Łopatka even warned the Warsaw Curia that unless the Church disciplined Father Popiełuszko and priests like him, it would be considered co-responsible for any breakdown in law and order.

The later court investigation reveals that apart from these two letters the subject of the "anti-state character" of Father Popiełuszko's services and sermons was raised during four special meetings between representatives of the Ministry for Religious Affairs and members of the Curia. All these meetings took place between January 1982 and August 1983. The Curia failed to oblige the Ministry; in any case, every sermon Father Popiełuszko preached was checked beforehand by one of Warsaw's auxiliary bishops and had an imprimatur from the Church.

Then a different tactic was adopted, that of openly putting pressure on Father Jerzy. Since the celebration of his first Mass for the Country he had been subjected to enormous pressure and was exposed to a great deal of intimidation. The St Stanisław Kostka presbytery was broken into and vandalized by "unknown hooligans" whom the police failed to track down. Twice his car was smeared with white paint. He was refused a passport to travel to Rome in October 1982 for the canonization of the Polish saint, Father Maximilian Kolbe – his own personal hero. Day and night he was constantly followed by security men. One day, when driving through the streets of Warsaw, he was asked by his passenger about the kind of intimidation he suffered. Father Jerzy turned on the car radio and after a while managed to find a frequency used by the security police. Suddenly, there was a secret "coded" message: "The wheels of the cross from Zoliborz have just passed." "There you are", he replied.[2]

Father Jerzy tried to ignore the fact that he was constantly followed. The only "tail" whose company he did enjoy was his little black mongrel dog. He had been a present to Father Jerzy in 1983, and was given the English name "Tiny" on account of his small size. "Tiny" pronounced by a Pole sounds very like "Tajniak" – the derogative term for a secret policeman – and, as Tiny followed Father Jerzy everywhere, he soon became "Tajniak", or "Tajniaczek", as Father Jerzy called him.

Father Jerzy loved his little dog dearly, but could only take him to see close friends, as Tiny, unlike his master, had an enormous appetite, and his favourite menu included soft furnishings and clothes!

Today, Tiny is well cared for by friends.

A priest who met Father Popiełuszko in Zarnowiec, on the Baltic coast, during his summer holiday in 1984, recalls how one day Father Jerzy pointed to two men innocently sunbathing nearby and said, "I know them. They were following me back in Warsaw." The day when Father Jerzy went to St Brygida's Church in Gdansk – the parish church of Lech Wałesa – the two "guardian angels" went with him and "brought him back" to the home of the Redemptorists' Order, where Father Jerzy was staying. On occasion the police would decide to "interrupt" journeys they considered politically provocative. In August 1983, while travelling to Gdansk, where he was to celebrate a Solidarity Mass together with Father Henryk Jankowski, Father Jerzy's car was stopped and he was kept at a police station outside Warsaw for eight hours. His driver was interrogated for fifty hours. The police thought that Father Popiełuszko was going to Gdansk to preach, but to the disappointment and fury of the interrogators no text of a sermon was found.

Father Jerzy was convinced that his telephone was bugged: again, he tried to take it lightheartedly. Whenever his conversation was interrupted by strange noises he would say, "Oh, that's nothing to worry about. A crow is probably sitting on the cable again." A crow – *wrona* in Polish – is a pun. *Wron*, the "Military Council of National Salvation", is an abbreviation widely used to describe General Jaruzelski's regime.

It was probably not until the night of 13th–14th December 1982, when a brick with a detonator inside it was thrown into the room next to his bedroom, that Father Jerzy really understood the danger he was facing. His doorbell rang but he did not answer it, and a moment later heard the breaking of glass. Then he opened his door and saw the brick with the detonator inside it. Although it did not explode, it was clear that the perpetrators had hoped that Father Jerzy would open the door and had then intended to throw this bomb at him. The incident shocked him. A friend who drove a relief lorry from England arrived the next morning, and recalls how Father Jerzy could not get over this act of violence. For him, a man filled with love, this act of hatred was incomprehensible. A month later, when another relief lorry arrived at St Stanisław Kostka Church, Father Jerzy was still talking about the incident.

After the episode of the brick, the Warsaw steel workers decided to organize protection for him. At first there were several men surrounding Father Jerzy day and night, but later the number gradually diminished, leaving only a few. Most of the people who visited Father Jerzy in his last year and a half usually recall the impressive figure of Mr Tadeusz, a retired steel man. A courageous and soft-hearted man, he could be hard on any unwelcome intruders. After a while Father Jerzy himself began to take the threat less seriously, however. When a friend met him last summer, all alone in the street outside the church and in a visible rush, she asked him reproachfully, "Why are you alone?" "Oh!" Father Jerzy explained, "but I'm only going to the dentist round the corner."

In time other priests began to join in the celebration of the Mass for the Country, to prove that Father Jerzy was not alone. When a plaque commemorating Solidarity was unveiled in St Stanisław Kostka Church in the summer of 1983, the parish priest, Father Teofil Bogucki, stressed publicly that the plaque was "my initiative, my endeavour and my responsibility". Such a public statement was not a form of boasting; it was intended to protect Father Jerzy. Only in May Father Jerzy had received an official letter accusing him of using language which was unbecoming in a church, at a Mass in the Holy Cross Church. Not only was Father Jerzy hearing confessions in St Stanisław Kostka Church on that day, but in fact he had never preached in the Holy Cross Church at all.

By the summer of 1983, the authorities tried to silence Father Popiełuszko by the threat of legal action. On 22nd September 1983, three days after the first workers' pilgrimage to Jasna Gora, where he led them through the "Stations of the Cross", an official investigation was ordered into Father Popiełuszko's alleged "abuse of freedom of conscience and religion". He was alleged to have "constantly included political slanders against the state authorities in his sermons: he claimed particularly that the authorities were violating human dignity and depriving society of freedom of thought and action through lies and anti-democratic laws". Thus "he was abusing the role of priest and was turning churches into places for anti-state propaganda, harmful to the interests of the Polish People's Republic" (Article 194 of the Polish Penal Code – this would carry a maximum sentence of fifteen years' imprisonment). The procurator in charge of his case had actually tried to summon Father Jerzy earlier so that he could be aware of the official accusation, but handing him a summons proved to be rather tricky. When, on 2nd December, a group of security men accompanied by an official from the procurator's office went to serve Father Popiełuszko with a summons, a nun working in the presbytery refused to accept it, as did the parish priest, and the men were referred to the Curia. Taking the summons to the Curia was no more successful. There, a priest read out the contents and passed it on to Bishop Władysław Miziołek, one of Warsaw's auxiliary bishops. The Bishop sent back a written reply. It explained that, as Cardinal Glemp was away, the Curia could not take an official position in the matter. Moreover, as the summons arrived after office hours, it was not possible to deal with the matter that day, and the priest in charge declined either to accept the summons or to pass it on to Father Popiełuszko; it was sent back.

On 12th December Father Jerzy went to the procurator's office accompanied by his two defence counsel, Messrs Wende and de Virion, as well as the parish priest, Father Teofil Bogucki, and a number of friends and well-wishers. The police were called in and the crowd was dispersed. Special check-points were set up, and everybody entering the building had to produce an identity card. Father Jerzy was faced with the "proofs of his crime" – tapes of the services, photographs and tapes of the Mass confiscated from an American TV network from Milwaukee.

According to Father Popiełuszko, the Ministry for Religious Affairs assured him that the whole interrogation would last one hour or so. However, after two hours the procurator told Father Jerzy that he had a warrant to search his flat. This did not worry Father Jerzy, as he knew that there was nothing incriminating there. When they all arrived at the flat, Father Jerzy was taken aback at the sight of the Polish TV car waiting for them. After three minutes the policemen "found" thousands of various *samizdat* (underground) leaflets divided into individual parcels and ready for distribution, thirty-eight pieces of ammunition and some explosives, including two hand grenades. It was interesting, according to Father Jerzy, that the policemen did not waste any time in searching but went straight to the places where the incriminating material was stored. One of the policemen seemed somehow to be familiar with the mechanism of Father Jerzy's sofa-bed, which was slightly damaged and needed to be opened in a special way.

Father Jerzy denied any knowledge of the "evidence" or of its origin, and at his request the search record stated that Father Popiełuszko considered the "findings" to be a provocation. The "sensational discovery" allowed the list of charges against him to be extended by Articles 143, 282 and 286 of the Polish Penal Code, i.e. producing and storing explosives, firearms and ammunition. They jointly carry a maximum penalty of twelve years' imprisonment. Father Jerzy was detained for the night and left to await the procurator's decision. The following day, during his weekly press conference with foreign journalists, the government spokesman, Jerzy Urban, disclosed that during the search of Father Popiełuszko's flat "a considerable number of objects providing serious legal evidence against Father Popiełuszko" had been found, but for some inexplicable reason he declined to give any further details. Was it because even he found the story difficult to believe? To defuse any suspicions of a possible provocation, Mr Urban also gave his own explanation for the search of Father Popiełuszko's flat. It was allegedly during the interrogation of 12th December 1983 that the authorities learnt of the flat's existence. But the address of the flat was written on Father Jerzy's identity card, which he had to produce every time he was stopped by the police, for example, on his way to Gdansk in August 1983. His "tail" had also accompanied Father Jerzy to the building where his flat was, and where his name featured on the list of tenants in the main entrance. Some light could have been thrown on the origin of the illegal material by the special TV/police camera crew, which, according to the KOS *samizdat* bulletin, was situated opposite Father Jerzy's flat for some time before 12th December. It transpires that the authorities chose not to use these crucial witnesses.

Later, during the trial of Father Jerzy's murderers, the main defendant, Captain Grzegorz Piotrowski, head of the section within the Church department of the Ministry for Religious Affairs, responsible for "limiting" the anti-state and anti-socialist activities of the Roman Catholic clergy, was to reveal a plan for intimidating Father Jerzy which gave further indication as to the origin of the incriminating material "found" in his flat. From time to time items would disappear from the flat, including money (all removed by the secret police), with the intention of making Father

Jerzy suspicious of his close friend, Waldemar Chrostowski, who often acted as Father Jerzy's driver and bodyguard, and who was the only other person to hold a key to the flat. Piotrowski reckoned that eventually Father Jerzy would distance himself from Chrostowski, and begin once more to travel alone. The secret police were able to "pay Father Jerzy a visit" at any time, providing, of course, that the host was not at home.

Father Jerzy spent the night of 12th–13th December in a cell which he shared with ordinary criminals. They treated Father Popiełuszko with respect, and by the time he left the prison at noon on 13th December he had heard the confession of one of the criminals. Shortly before his death, Father Jerzy revealed to a foreign visitor that on that night in the cell he found his main comfort in the thought that so many people were praying for him both in Poland and abroad.

He was released following the intervention of Archbishop Bronisław Dabrowski, the Secretary of the Polish Episcopate. On his release Father Jerzy was warned, however, that the authorities' attitude towards him would depend on his own future attitude. He realized then that the whole incident was not only designed to discredit him in the eyes of the Polish Episcopate and people. It was also a stark warning that nothing was impossible for the Polish authorities, regardless of whether it was credible or not.

Father Popiełuszko's friends and superiors advised him to take a long holiday in the mountains, which was in any case justifiable and even necessary because of his bad health. On 18th December a statement from Father Jerzy was read out during every Mass at St Stanisław Kostka Church. In it he explained that he had a small flat, given to him by his aunt five years earlier, of whose existence the Church authorities had been informed. In this flat had been found items whose origin was unknown to him. "Their nature, when compared with my widely known pastoral activities, is a total absurdity. I consider this a provocation." The accusations of the authorities were also rejected categorically by Father Teofil Bogucki. In his sermon on Christmas Eve he described Father Jerzy as a man "who spread love" at a time of "prevailing hatred and falsehood". Thousands of people came to the St Stanisław Kostka Church on 25th December, for the December Mass for the Country celebrated by Father Popiełuszko. Their presence was the best way of showing the authorities how the people judged the so-called "sensational discovery".

For Father Jerzy his most trying time had begun. Between January and June 1984 he was interrogated thirteen times. Intimidation was stepped up, and included Father Popiełuszko's friends and even casual visitors. Cars parked outside his presbytery were often vandalized, and his visitors questioned by the police. On 17th September 1984 Mirosława Polankiewicz was sacked from her work simply because she had accompanied Father Jerzy to the procurator's office and tried to watch the procedures from her own office window, which was located opposite. Waldemar Chrostowski – his friend, driver and bodyguard – was interrogated and pressured "to cease the friendship". When Chrostowski ignored the warnings his flat was mysteriously burnt out in September 1984. Even the plastic ventilators in the kitchen had melted, suggesting that a highly inflammable substance had been used – possibly something similar to napalm, which of course could only have come from the state military warehouse.

Father Jerzy found the constant interrogation very trying, and always asked his friends to pray for him. Sometimes he would even announce the date of the interrogation during the Mass for the Country, and also ask the people for a special prayer. There were, however, a few occasions when he joked about these meetings with the authorities. "I am not afraid," he said to one of his friends, "let them arrest me. The crowd of believers will come with me. They'll sit down outside the secret police headquarters and sing all the litanies they know." Father Jerzy was always accompanied on his way to interrogation by a crowd of people who waited for him outside. When he appeared after interrogation Father Jerzy was welcomed enthusiastically by the waiting crowd, which had been enlarged by numerous office workers tipped off by look-outs standing at the windows of offices adjacent to the Ministry of the Interior. The authorities were clearly infuriated by these scenes right outside their sacred work place. In the later indictment Father Jerzy was also charged with "using the interrogation as a chance to cause public unrest". His disclosure of the dates of the interrogations during the Masses for the Country was also considered a crime. According to the indictment "it resulted in a group of people accompanying Father Popiełuszko on his way to the interrogation and waiting for him at the front door. This group caused public disorder and a crowd gathering in front of the city council of the Ministry of the Interior." Once, after an especially long interrogation, Father Jerzy appeared and confessed to a friend, "I almost told them how many working hours are wasted merely because people don't know when I'll be coming out."

Father Jerzy was enjoying increasing prestige and respect even among people outside the Church. According to reports, some local policemen refused to participate in persecuting him, and men from outside Warsaw had to be used. One day the nun working in the St Stanisław Kostka Church refused to accept a letter for Father Jerzy, and sent the man to the Curia office at Miodowa Street. The man seemed not to have a clue as to where this well-known Warsaw street was, and finally asked some parishioners for guidance; he was obviously not from Warsaw. Father Popiełuszko himself recalled how one Friday evening he was hearing confessions in the church when someone came to tell him that secret policemen were waiting for him outside the presbytery. When he had finished hearing confessions, Father Jerzy left the church and walked towards the presbytery. On passing the policemen one of them asked him, "Do you know Father Popiełuszko?" "Yes, a little", he answered and went indoors.

His closest friends knew how painful this intimidation and the charges brought against him were for Father Jerzy. "How on earth *can* freedom of conscience be violated?" he would ask them despairingly. Father Jerzy was incapable of hatred. To cite an example illustrating this, there was a time when on Christmas Eve 1981, two weeks into martial law, he went outside after the curfew to break the traditional Polish wafer bread with the ZOMO police. Now, anyone outside at this time was liable to be shot on sight. However, he still approached these notorious police, in his civilian clothes, and his gesture was reciprocated by some in their ranks who broke and ate the wafer bread with him. During those first two weeks of martial law these same ZOMO police had been the perpetrators of horrific violence against Solidarity members and indeed against ordinary citizens right across the nation. Truly, this gesture of Father Jerzy's was an extreme example of "loving thine enemy".

He was, however, deeply saddened that his life's vocation, his pastoral work, could be classed as "subversive activity". What worried him most was that the people who persecuted him, still his brothers in Christ and his fellow countrymen, remained in the service of evil, in the darkness, untouched by the love of God.

During this whole trying time Father Jerzy received all possible moral support from two auxiliary Warsaw bishops – Władysław Miziołek and Zbigniew Kraszewski. They defended him courageously and tirelessly against all accusations. Father Popiełuszko also enjoyed the approval of the Polish Pope, John Paul II; through Bishop Kraszewski, the Pope had in February 1984 sent him a rosary as a token of his esteem and in recognition of his pastoral work: "Please tell him that I am with him, with all my heart." His mother recalls how happy and proud Father Jerzy was with his Papal gift. He brought it home to show to his parents and considered it his greatest treasure. Father Jerzy never saw another gift from the Pope – a cross – which arrived in Warsaw the day after his kidnapping. It was later given to Father Jerzy's parents and now hangs in their home in Okopy.

In the last year or so the Pope had also sent Father Jerzy greetings through parish pilgrims, and had asked visiting Poles to give him up-to-date news on his case. This overt sign of John Paul II's interest in Father Jerzy's fate made many people feel that fears for his safety must be exaggerated. Even in the summer of 1984 a Polish priest tried to persuade me that nothing could really happen to Father Jerzy with such a protector in the Vatican. How wrong he was. The vicious campaign against Father Jerzy was escalating dramatically, especially after the May Mass for the Country.

With just three weeks to the municipal elections, which the authorities hoped to use as proof of "normalization" within Poland, Father Popiełuszko warned his congregation: "We ourselves are responsible for our slavery, when either through fear or the desire for an untroubled life, we elect authorities who proceed to promote evil. If we vote such people into power then we have no right to condemn evil, as we ourselves help to create it and to legalize it."

On 12th July an indictment against Father Jerzy was made out by the Warsaw deputy procurator and addressed to the Warsaw regional court. Father Jerzy was charged with the abuse of freedom of conscience and religion, to the detriment of the Polish People's Republic; with storing for the purpose of distribution various illegal publications whose content slandered and humiliated the "supreme organs of the state authorities"; and with possession of ammunition and explosives without permission (Articles 194, 286, 143 and 282a of the Polish Penal Code).

On 29th July, during the Mass for the Country, Father Teofil Bogucki took the unprecedented step of publicly defending Father Jerzy in a sermon. This was an extraordinary sermon – quite different from the kind that people normally expect to hear in church. It was a sermon about Father Popiełuszko, a kind of apologia and in places even a eulogy. Such a sermon seemed, however, completely justifiable in the circumstances. Father Bogucki himself explained that he considered it his "duty in the capacity of parish priest, in the face of false charges, to point to Father Jerzy's shining personality". He considered Father Jerzy "one of the best priests I know – full of the Holy Spirit, and also one of the best Poles – noble and devoted to his country with his whole heart . . . Everybody is a witness that he has never preached feelings of hate or revenge . . . Yes," said Father Bogucki bitterly, "one can make a criminal out of anybody and prove his guilt if one ignores one's conscience and public opinion, or uses any means possible . . .

"Father Jerzy is not an anarchist. He calls for peace, wisdom and patience. This proves the peaceful and serious nature of our Masses for the Country. Father Jerzy comforts distressed minds and helps them to get rid of anxiety." And he added in words which have an almost unbearable poignancy today, "All of us pray night and day for Father Jerzy, trusting that no one in Poland will ever harm him."

All charges against Father Jerzy were suspended under the amnesty marking the fortieth anniversary of communist Poland. The official notification of this came to him very late. While in Warsaw rumours were spreading of Father Jerzy's exclusion from the amnesty, he received open backing from the Church. On 21st August Bishop Władysław Miziołek delivered a sermon in St Stanisław Kostka Church during a special thanksgiving Mass for the prisoners pardoned under the amnesty. At a time when the official line of the Church requested people to refrain from such Masses, the Bishop's presence acquired great significance. In a strongly worded sermon, Bishop Miziołek stated: "Nobody should be imprisoned for his political beliefs, everybody should have the right to express his opinions freely." Three days later the authorities decided to include Father Popiełuszko's case in the amnesty, but it was not until 28th August that the letter finally reached him. It was clear that news of his amnesty brought relief to Father Jerzy. However, he knew all too well that in reality it was just a postponement of the inevitable case against him. Under the terms of the amnesty, he had to refrain from similar "political actions" for two and a half years; the cancellation of the charges depended on this. It would mean the cessation of the Masses for the Country, and Father Jerzy would not allow this to happen. On 26th August, two days before the official notification of the amnesty reached him, he had already preached again, thus risking the possibility of his case being reopened. He appealed to the people once more to uphold the hopes of 1980 and to overcome fear.

In the autumn of 1984 Father Jerzy even had "the honour" of becoming known in Moscow. On 12th September of that year, in a correspondent's report from Warsaw, *Izvestia* carried a slanderous attack on him. A Russian journalist, who apparently considered himself an expert on theology, gave his opinion of Father Jerzy's sermons. "Recently . . . Father Popiełuszko turned to those pardoned under the amnesty with this message: 'You've had a rest and now it is high time to go back to work. The most important thing is not to be afraid.' The priest is not afraid. He turned his flat into a warehouse for illegal literature; he co-operates closely with desperate counter-revolutionaries. One gets the impression that he does not read sermons from the pulpit but rather leaflets written by Bujak [formerly regional Solidarity leader, now leader of the Underground Solidarity, in hiding since 13th December 1981]. They breathe out hatred of socialism."

Only a week later, on 19th September, Jerzy Urban, the government spokesman, using his pen-name of "Jan Rem", joined in a scathing attack on Father Jerzy. In an article entitled "Seances of Hate", Urban described Father Popiełuszko as a "political magician", "the Savonarola of anti-communism", who organized "seances of hate", "black masses" in which nothing new or interesting is said, but in which the priest "manipulates collective emotions".

Three days before Urban's attack, on 16th September, in the Warsaw church of St Joseph, Father Jerzy was nominated a regional chaplain of the working people in recognition of his pastoral work. The news was later publicized in Polish *samizdat*. It was a very welcome gesture; in the last few months of his life Father Jerzy needed moral support from the people as never before.

Urban's article contained a crucial statement which reveals the true reason for Father Jerzy's persecution: he admitted that a struggle for the Polish soul is taking place in Poland today, even though "nothing like a human soul really exists". Father Jerzy was indeed fighting a battle for the souls of his people, but he fought precisely because he *did* believe in the soul's existence, in the life to come. Father Popiełuszko's only "guilt" was that he tried tirelessly to bring people to Christ, and through Christ to God. In mutual service they would then begin to build a "living Church". Back in 1976 Pope John Paul II, then still Cardinal Karol Wojtyła of Krakow, whilst conducting a retreat for members of the Vatican Curia, had said: "We are living in an age in which the whole world proclaims freedom of conscience and religious freedom, and also in an age in which the battle against religion – defined as 'the opium of the people' – is being fought in such a way as to avoid, as far as possible, making any new martyrs. And so the programme for today is one of face-saving persecution; persecution is declared 'non-existent' and full religious freedom is declared and assured. What is more, this programme has succeeded in giving many people the impression that it is on the side of Lazarus against the rich man, that it is therefore on the same side as Christ, whereas in fact it is above all *against* Christ. Can we really say, 'above all'? We would so much like to be able to affirm the opposite. But unfortunately the facts demonstrate clearly that the battle against religion is being fought, and this battle still constitutes an immovable point of dogma in the programme. It also seems as if, for the attainment of this 'heaven on earth', it is most of all necessary to deprive man of the strength he draws on in Christ. This 'strength' has indeed been condemned as weakness, unworthy of man. Unworthy . . . troublesome, rather. The man who is strong with the strength given him by the faith does not easily allow himself to be thrust into the anonymity of the collective."

Father Jerzy was convinced that communist, atheist ideology was the real danger facing not only the Church but the whole of humanity. He believed that the real conflict of the twentieth century was not between the Eastern and Western blocs, not even between the rich and the poor. The real conflict lay between two world outlooks: the religious outlook with its transcendental vision of man, and materialistic nihilism – a struggle between the concept of "love thy neighbour" and the concept of the class struggle. If the authorities saw Father Popiełuszko – an ordinary priest – as their main enemy, it was because of his uncompromising Christianity. It was because he ignored all the unwritten rules and "dared" to preach the Gospel openly, in a straightforward manner, in the light of contemporary experience. It was the fact that he had built this "solidarity of hearts", a community of people who had experienced inner freedom, that posed the greatest danger to the authorities, and in this lay the reason for Father Popiełuszko's martyrdom.

By the summer of 1984 the workers of Warsaw's steel plant were convinced that Father Jerzy's pastoral work would inevitably lead to further repressions, and in a dramatic move they asked the Church to save their priest. In a letter handed to Archbishop Dabrowski, the Secretary of the Polish Episcopate, they stated: "Four years of Father Jerzy's pastoral work among the workers . . . have gathered thousands of Warsaw workers around the parish of St Stanisław Kostka at Zoliborz. During the especially difficult period, when we were imprisoned, interned, beaten up and provoked, thanks to Father Jerzy we understood that we had to reject violence and the desire for vengeance as they are non-Christian forms of the struggle for human rights and dignity. Thanks to Father Jerzy we replaced those feelings with love and prayer for those who wronged us . . . Unfortunately Father Jerzy's activities among the workers are not appreciated by the present state authorities. By the use of methods known to us – provocation, slander, blackmail and even attempts to endanger his life – he has been officially charged. The political situation in the country does not favour any radical protests, as these could be used by provocateurs; therefore we limited ourselves to sending a protest to the Polish Parliament when news of the indictment reached us. The amnesty of 22nd July, which apparently will also include Father Jerzy on conditions known to everybody, makes us workers morally responsible for him. After many conversations between ourselves, we have decided that if it is possible the best solution would be to send Father Jerzy abroad for study."

Cardinal Glemp found himself in a very difficult position. If he sent Father Jerzy abroad it would look to outsiders like exile. At a time when the Polish authorities were contemplating the forcible emigration of all unwanted political opponents, such a move on the part of the Church could give them a welcome precedent. On the other hand, on no account would Father Jerzy himself request even temporary leave. He felt that this would mean the betrayal of all the people who looked up to him. In time Father Jerzy began to look favourably on the idea of a temporary stay in Rome. He felt very responsible for his ministry, and worried whether he had already said everything he could to the people. In Rome he felt he would have so much time to study the Church's social thought that later, after his return to Poland, he could share his newly acquired knowledge with the people. He was also happy at the prospect of seeing Rome, for after Niepokalanow, Rome was his second most loved town. Friends recall how heartbroken he was when the authorities refused him a passport to travel to Rome for the canonization of Maximilian Kolbe. Those who were lucky enough to be in Rome were later constantly "pestered" by Father Jerzy to talk about the See of St Peter.

While the organization of his departure for Rome dragged on over the summer, Father Jerzy still agonized over his decision of whether to go or not. Those most close to him offer conflicting versions of his final decision. We know that shortly before his abduction, he learnt that the final arrangements for his trip were being made. This prompted some of his friends later to see his murder as the inevitable conclusion of the satanic hatred felt for him by the secret police. It was precipitated by his plans for going to Rome because, in their opinion, he might not return and would therefore escape their "punishment". After his murder, posters of Father Popiełuszko appeared all over Rome. Someone managed to smuggle a few back to Poland. When they were put up just outside his room a friend remarked, "So, Jerzy, you went to Rome after all."

For some time before his kidnapping it was apparent to his close friends that Father Jerzy certainly was, on a human level, afraid of what might happen to him. They noticed that he began to smoke much more than usual. Those who visited him found him changed; he had matured and was certainly bowed under the enormous burden. One of Father Jerzy's admirers, who came to all his Masses in St Stanisław Kostka Church, remarked that "the shadow of the Cross was so visible on Father Jerzy's face" that she could not bear it and stopped attending the Masses. She was not alone in noticing the look on his face. There were also times when Father Jerzy seemed to be unable to take the pressure any more. One hot August day, he and a few close friends were walking through the streets of Warsaw when he suddenly turned to them and said, "Listen, let's go to the seaside." They were taken aback. Father Jerzy – this workaholic, and such a crazy idea! They looked at his white, tired face and did not say a word. After a few minutes he seemed to forget about the sea and they returned to the church.

The constant tension was probably accountable for the

fact that in the last year of his life he decided to rent an allotment in the parish garden. He would try to spend every possible moment of free time there tending his plot. Perhaps during these moments he would be at one with his home farm back in Okopy.

Did Father Jerzy fear death? Did he think of himself when he heard the words of the psalm spoken during the Mass for the Country? –

> Take pity on me, God, as they harm me,
> pressing their attacks home all day.
> All day my opponents harm me,
> hordes are coming to my attack . . .
> All day long they twist what I say,
> all they think is how to harm me.
> They conspire, lurk, spy on my movements,
> determined to take my life.
>
> (Psalm 56:1–2, 5–6)

In his last two weeks several incidents occurred which suggested that Father Jerzy took the possibility of his death very seriously. His September visit to his parents – his last visit – differed from all the others. Father Jerzy stayed longer than usual, and before leaving he walked round the whole house and the farm as if he wanted to say goodbye to all the memories of his childhood. When a friend visited him in September, he found Father Jerzy engrossed in writing. "I am making my will", Father Jerzy informed him. "Do you want anything specific?" The friend looked at him in amazement and promised, "I'll think about it and let you know!" The will was never found. On another day he decided to shift his furniture around and tidy up his room. He was pleased with the results, and said to a passing nun, "What a pity that I shan't enjoy it for long." At the time she thought that Father Jerzy had his trip to Rome in mind, and did not pay much attention to his words. The incident came back to her with a new meaning after Father Jerzy's body was found. On another occasion he explained,

"Even if I am afraid, I cannot act otherwise. In fact I'd only be afraid if what I was doing was wrong . . . and then we always live with the risk of death. If we must die it is better to meet death while defending a worthwhile cause than sitting back and letting an injustice take place."[3] "In the history of Christianity we have many examples showing us to what extent the truth has to be defended – quite simply, to the end: Jesus Christ for preaching God's truth gave His life; similarly the apostles. After all, the priest is called to bear witness to the truth, to suffer for the truth and if need be to give up his life for it. We have many such examples in Christianity. From them we should draw conclusions for ourselves."[4]

According to Waldemar Chrostowski, Father Jerzy did not feel trapped. He tried to behave naturally, even though the danger was apparent. A week before the kidnapping, when they were returning from Gdansk to Warsaw, a man suddenly appeared from the forest at the side of the road. He carried something heavy in his hand and tried to throw it at the car. Chrostowski turned the car sharply towards him, the assailant panicked, tripped over and missed the car. They decided that he must have been "a madman". Chrostowski was not to know that it was only his quick reaction that saved not only Father Jerzy's life that day – 13th October – but also his own and that of their other passenger, Seweryn Jaworski, the former vice-chairman of the regional Solidarity of Mazowsze. For it was not the attempt of a madman, it was a preplanned plot to kill Father Popiełuszko, along with the two other people accompanying him, which failed at the last moment.

After 13th October Father Jerzy was living on borrowed time; his fate was sealed. A few weeks earlier a special meeting in the Ministry of the Interior had been called by Adam Pietruszka, the deputy head of the Ministry's religious affairs department. Apart from Pietruszka, those present included Grzegorz Piotrowski – the head of the department's inner section concerned with monitoring "anti-state" and "anti-socialist" actions by members of the

Roman Catholic Church – and Leszek Wolski, head of the Warsaw security office. Pietruszka, on orders from above – as he alleged – stated that it was high time to stop toying with "anti-state" priests, and urged "decisive and speedy action". In the discussion that followed, Father Popiełuszko was singled out as the first priest who had to be dealt with. Piotrowski eagerly agreed to take this "task" upon himself, as he was later to describe it. He had many personal reasons for "getting his own back" on Father Popiełuszko. After all, it was he who was in charge of gathering evidence against Father Jerzy, and he had felt very frustrated when the "available forms and methods" of intimidating the priest had failed. Shortly after the meeting, Piotrowski set up a "working operational group", consisting of himself and his two subordinates – Leszek Pekala and Waldemar Chmielewski. Both were chosen, according to Piotrowski, for their physical fitness and their good working record. Even in court, Piotrowski still claimed that the feelings towards Father Popiełuszko were so hostile within the department that "If I had shouted out asking who wanted to take part in an operation against Father Popiełuszko, many would have volunteered." However, there was no need for this, as both Pekala and Chmielewski agreed to take part in the "action". In court Pekala stated without hesitation that he had hoped it would further his career. Chmielewski was allegedly influenced by "official loyalty". All three perpetrators of the crime were absolutely convinced that they were acting within the framework of an important task, which came from the "very top". They were also sure of their full immunity before the law.

Because of often vague and contradictory statements later made in court by all the perpetrators of the crime and by the witnesses, it is impossible to establish a completely true version of the events leading up to the murder of Father Popiełuszko. The first plan was to kidnap and hold Father Jerzy in a wartime bunker in Kampinos forest just outside Warsaw, in order to intimidate him into giving up his activities and disclosing the names of underground activists and their whereabouts. The second plan was to take him to a bridge on the Wisła river and hang him over it in order to frighten him, for the same reasons. A third plan, unsuccessfully put into practice on 13th October, was to stone the car, make it crash, and then burn it and its occupants. Twenty litres of petrol were acquired for the purpose.

It was not only in the third plan that Father Jerzy's death figured. In fact in all the plans the question of his death was taken into account. According to Pekala, Piotrowski not only considered the possibility of Father Jerzy dying in the course of "persuasive talks" but he saw his death as their ultimate goal. The choice of methods at their disposal seemed to be vast – ranging from pushing him out of a train, to digging a hole in the ground in a wood, tying up the priest, putting him into the hole, filling it with soil up to his neck and then covering his head with branches, so that he would die of a combination of exposure, exhaustion and starvation. Piotrowski saw Father Popiełuszko's death simply as the most convincing "warning" to other "political" priests, one which would also make the Polish Church "more amenable" in its dealings with the authorities.

Whatever Father Jerzy felt and thought of the incident on 13th October, he was not prepared to be intimidated. In the sermon he preached five days after Father Jerzy's murder, Bishop Kraszewski recalled the friendly warnings he had tried to convey to the priest just before his death. Father Jerzy had listened to the Bishop's words of concern with a holy smile on his face, and the Bishop saw in his eyes "the light of joy, the joy of the servant who is always ready".

1 *Tydziew Polski*, 10th November 1984.
2 Zoliborz was the district in which Father Popiełuszko worked.
3 Unpublished interview.
4 Unpublished interview.

# 6

# The Crime of Cain

On Friday 19th October 1984 Father Popiełuszko was expected in Bydgoszcz, a town in northern Poland, some two hundred and fifty-nine kilometres from Warsaw. He had been invited to take part in a special Mass for "the working people" by Father Jerzy Osinski, vicar of the parish of the Polish Brother Martyrs. On the day his friends tried to talk him out of it, as Father Jerzy had a very bad cold with a high temperature. Moreover, Professor Klemens Szaniawski, who was supposed to accompany him on the journey, could not leave Warsaw that day. But Father Jerzy insisted on going – he did not want to let the people down.

At about 9.30 a.m. he left for Bydgoszcz in a car driven by his friend Waldemar Chrostowski. Marek Wilk, a representative of the Bydgoszcz parish, followed in another car, as escort. Outside Warsaw Father Popiełuszko's car was stopped by the traffic police. After a short conversation he was allowed to continue the journey and both cars arrived at Bydgoszcz at about two o'clock. At 6 p.m., together with Father Osinski, Father Jerzy began the celebration of what was to be his last Mass. Father Osinski had been threatened by the local security police with "serious consequences" if he allowed Father Popiełuszko to preach. Father Jerzy did not want to get him into any trouble so, instead of a sermon, the people were invited to stay behind after the Mass, and participate in the sorrowful mysteries of the rosary, led by Father Popiełuszko. There was nothing unusual about this as October, a month dedicated to Mary in the Catholic tradition, is observed strictly in Poland. Each of the five mysteries was preceded by a short meditation by Father Popiełuszko. The main theme of all five was "overcome evil with good". His last words to the congregation were, "Let us pray that we may be free from fear and intimidation, but most of all that we may be free from the desire for violence and vengeance."

As Father Popiełuszko said these words, his three murderers – Piotrowski, Pekala and Chmielewski – were already waiting for him in the car just outside the presbytery. They had arrived in Bydgoszcz that same afternoon, determined not to repeat the failure of 13th October. In addition to two sacks filled with stones they had also acquired wooden clubs (cut in the forest on their way to Bydgoszcz), handcuffs, a traffic policeman's uniform, ropes, gauze and – most essential for their plans – "a W Pass", which allowed them to ignore all traffic regulations and exempted them from any control. They did not act in secrecy, far from it. On their arrival in Bydgoszcz they paid a visit to the local security police office and made official calls to Warsaw. They expressed no concern whatsoever when the local policeman noticed that they had changed the registration plate on their car and wrote down the new number. "Let them write", Piotrowski shrugged his shoulders in disdain.

In the meantime the rosary had ended and a group of parishioners followed Father Jerzy to the presbytery, where they had a short chat. By this time Father Popiełuszko's temperature had gone up again. He felt ill and hardly spoke during the supper prepared for him. Some of those present tried to persuade him to go to bed and leave for Warsaw the following day, after at least a night's rest, but Father Jerzy would not hear of it. He knew that he was expected to say the early morning Mass at St Stanisław Kostka Church, and his absence would inconvenience the two other priests at a time when the parish priest, Father Teofil Bogucki, was in hospital. Father Jerzy also declined the suggestion that Marek Wilk should escort them back to Warsaw. Instead he asked him to lead them to the outskirts of town and put them on the road leading to Torun. Just before their departure for Warsaw, he asked one of the group at the presbytery, who was returning to Białystok, to take a gift to his mother – a picture of Our Lady of Jasna Gora against a black background. After a brief farewell, Father Popiełuszko went out to the car which Chrostowski had brought round from the garage, and they set off, following Marek Wilk in his car. Several people noticed two other cars which went after them, one of them a Fiat. On the outskirts of the town, Marek Wilk stopped, pointed to the Torun highway, and turned back home. One of the two cars which had followed them from the presbytery then turned round and followed him; the Fiat drove on behind Father Popiełuszko's Volkswagen.

The distance from Bydgoszcz to Torun is exactly forty-seven kilometres. After about fifteen kilometres Chrostowski noticed that they were being followed. As in the last three years they had become so used to this, there was no reason to suspect anything out of the ordinary. Suddenly the car behind closed up on them and overtook. Inside they noticed a traffic policeman flashing a red light at them. The Fiat stopped on the right. A policeman stretched his hand out of the window and waved at them with a torch, warning them to stop. Chrostowski decided to ignore the order. The car had no official markings. Moreover it had early on been decided that they would not stop in such a situation unless there were other civilian witnesses present. Father Jerzy, however, told him to stop. "It's not worth risking possible trouble", he said. Maybe, thinking of the brief police check-up that morning on the way to Bydgoszcz, he foresaw a spate of "controls" as the new form of intimidation to be directed against him.

Chrostowski stopped in front of the Fiat. He didn't know that at that moment the four stations of Father Jerzy's own way of the Cross were beginning – as one of the prosecutors said later in the trial. The officer quickly came up to their car. He ordered Chrostowski to hand him the car keys and to follow him to the police car for a breathalyser. Once inside the Fiat, instead of being given the test, Chrostowski was swiftly handcuffed, gagged and held at gun point. He saw that this was not a traffic check-up but a preplanned assault on Father Popiełuszko. Chrostowski thought of throwing himself onto the car horn in order to warn his friend, but soon realized that Father Jerzy stood no chance of fighting off three physically fit men, and that such action would enrage them. He decided to keep calm and wait for a suitable opportunity to act.

A plain-clothes policeman got out of the back seat of the Fiat and, together with the "police officer", went towards the Volkswagen. After a moment, Chrostowski saw Father Popiełuszko getting out of the car and walking towards the Fiat. Halfway he stopped and hesitated. There was some pushing and shoving, and Chrostowski heard Father Jerzy say, "Gentlemen, what are you doing, how can you behave like this? This is an assault." Father Popiełuszko was dragged to the back of the Fiat, where the policemen first used their fists and a wooden club to beat him into unconsciousness. Then, although he was unconscious, he was tied up, gagged and thrown into the boot. They slammed it shut and jumped into the car. Chrostowski already had a rope round his neck and was now informed that this would be his "last journey". Soon after, the driver was ordered to turn into the woods.

Chrostowski knew that he had to act immediately. He thought of grabbing the steering wheel as soon as the car was going sufficiently fast to cause an accident and so overturn the car. He soon gave up that idea, keeping it as a last resort. As he couldn't turn round, he was not sure whether Father Jerzy was really in the boot or whether a heavy sack had been thrown in to deceive him. Maybe Father Jerzy had been left on the road unconscious; maybe someone else had been waiting to take him away for "questioning". If, however, there was a possibility that Father Jerzy actually was in the boot and unconscious, then he certainly would not come out alive from an accident.

Chrostowski decided to try to jump out of the car, at a time when there were witnesses around. He was very much aware that such a jump meant the possibility of death, but his only concern was to leave some sort of clue, so that someone would react to it. He leaned forward in the seat, felt the door handle with his little finger, and waited for a suitable moment. Suddenly he saw a small Fiat car which they had just overtaken, and on the left-hand side of the road, two men standing near a motorcycle. This was his opportunity. He decided to jump into the path of the little Fiat's headlights, so that its passengers would see exactly what was going on. He pulled the door handle, threw himself at the door, shoulder first – and it flew open. Someone in the car tried to hold him back but was left holding just a piece of torn clothing. The handcuffs came open during his fall. After he had stopped rolling, to break his fall, he got up to his feet and ran to the road. He tried desperately to stop the little Fiat, but the driver drove away. Chrostowski did not know that close by, in Fordon, there was a high-security prison; in his state the occupants of the small car could have taken him for an escaped convict.

When the little Fiat had disappeared, Chrostowski ran towards the two men beside the motorcycle. He told them what had happened and begged them to follow the Fiat, or at least go back to check whether Father Jerzy had been left by the side of the road. The motorcycle had broken down, but the men directed him to a large, well-lit building – a local farming centre. He ran there to telephone for help. A group of men took him to the caretaker's room. She was clearly frightened by Chrostowski's tattered appearance, handcuffs dangling from one hand, and holding the piece of rope. Once again he explained what had happened, that they had been attacked, that Father Jerzy had been kidnapped and that she must contact the Warsaw Curia or the Episcopate immediately. The caretaker was unable to get through to Warsaw, so Chrostowski asked her to telephone the nearest church. He also asked for an ambulance – only now was he beginning to feel the effects of the fall. She did as he asked, and also decided to ring the police in Torun. A local policeman arrived on a motorcycle after the ambulance taking Chrostowski had gone. The doctor diagnosed bruises, external abrasion of the left side of the body, injury to the left knee, a twisted right ankle joint, and a fracture of the articular capsule. Chrostowski asked the doctor to take him immediately to any local priest and the doctor took him to the church of the Holy Virgin.

It was now about 11 p.m., and Father Jozef Nowakowski was going to bed when he heard the door bell. In front of the presbytery stood an ambulance. Father Nowakowski was told that the patient wanted to see the priest. He let him in. At first Chrostowski could not gather his thoughts together and just kept repeating, "Save Father Jerzy, save the priest." He tried to describe the order of events but was so muddled that Father Nowakowski even thought that this was police provocation of some kind. Chrostowski had his work pass on him, and the priest asked him to recite all the personal data on it from memory. In the end he no longer had any doubts: the resident priest of St Stanisław Kostka Church, Father Jerzy Popiełuszko, had been kidnapped. Father Nowakowski rang the police and informed them of the incident, stressing the presence of the man in police uniform. He then accompanied Chrostowski to the hospital. The police were already there. Chrostowski was immediately taken to the police station for interrogation. It lasted till dawn. Then he was taken to the hospital of the Ministry of the Interior – in a section allocated for prisoners. After leaving Chrostowski, Father Nowakowski decided to drive out and check whether Father Popiełuszko was still lying by the side of the road. When he arrived at the spot policemen were there, securing the Volkswagen. There was no trace of Father Jerzy.

When Chrostowski jumped out of the Fiat at the little village of Przesiek, Captain Piotrowski simply gave the order to drive on. After a while Father Popiełuszko regained consciousness, and began to bang on the boot and to shout loudly. They decided to stop and tie him down more firmly, choosing some open ground close to the Wisła river where they could do this unnoticed. By the time they had got out of the car, Father Popiełuszko was running away, shouting for help. He was about ten metres from the car when they caught him. Piotrowski beat him again and again with the wooden club. He pleaded, "Please spare my life", but as the beating continued Father Popiełuszko became silent – he was unconscious. Gagged and tied down more thoroughly, he was bundled again into the boot of the Fiat. They changed the registration plate of the car back to the original one, and drove off towards Włocławek. Father Popiełuszko survived this beating, regained consciousness and again began to try to prise the lid of the boot open. The car pulled over to the cover of some bushes. Pekala was driving slowly, and both Piotrowski and Chmielewski were running alongside the car holding down its boot. Piotrowski, "outraged" by Father Popiełuszko's "lack of obedience" – as he would later say in court – was "forced" to beat him again. These increasingly serious blows were inflicted on Father Jerzy whilst he was still huddled in the boot. Piotrowski's fury was such that he threatened to "strangle the priest" with his bare hands. Father Jerzy was then dragged out of the boot and beaten again. The bindings on his hands and legs were tightened, a gag was pushed further into his mouth, and he was put back into the boot. They returned to the main road, at which point Piotrowski gave the order to look for the nearest wood.

After only a few minutes, they found a wood and drove deep into it. Father Jerzy was again taken out of the boot of the car; by this time there was very little movement in him. He was laid on a blanket, then Pekala and Chmielewski proceeded to tie him up in a particularly lethal manner. The rope was wound several times around one leg and then, at ankle level, was wound once again around the other leg, which meant that the legs were bound separately and in a figure of eight. A separate rope attached to the legs ran along the spine to the neck and was looped around it. In this way, if the legs were moved to straighten up, the loop around the throat would become tighter, and would strangle Father Jerzy. At this point, yet more gagging material was pushed into his mouth and sealed with a strip of sticking plaster some fifty centimetres long. Over the plaster the men placed another layer of gauze, which was itself fastened by another layer of plaster around the neck and covering the nose. The net effect of all this was that Father Jerzy's breathing was severely obstructed. Piotrowski ordered, "Stones to his legs!" A heavy bag was then attached to each leg and he was bundled back into the boot. The three abductors returned to the main road. Piotrowski gave the order to head for the dam on the Wisła river. On the way the car was in its turn stopped by a police car, but they waved their special "W Pass" which exempted them from any traffic control, and carried on until they reached the dam. Together they dragged Father Jerzy to this dam on the Włocławek reservoir and threw him, weighted down with the bags of stones, into the water. According to the final statement of the forensic experts at the trial, he could – even then – have still been alive.

In court these experts stated that it was the maltreatment suffered by the priest that led to his death. Father Jerzy died as a result of the beatings he received, of the gags and of strangulation. In the opinion of the forensic experts, Father Jerzy already began to die during the third "stop" in the bushes. The previous beatings led to a serious impairment of his circulatory and respiratory system. He was already in a state of shock. The injuries sustained and the pain linked with them during the first two beatings were, however, still of a reversible nature, because the body was able to mobilize its mechanisms of adaptation and regulation. As the beating continued and asphyxiation increased, his body began to enter into a state of irreversible shock, with the successive anoxaemia of the organs essential for life – the brain, the heart, the lungs and the kidneys. We shall never know for certain whether

Father Jerzy's body survived this state of profound anoxaemia, and thus whether he was still alive when he was thrown into the reservoir, or whether he was already dead. As far as the three security men were concerned their task had been completed "successfully". They returned to Warsaw.

The official announcement about the abduction was made the following day, Saturday 20th October, on the main evening news at 7.30 p.m. It was later repeated several times. Shortly after the first communiqué people started to arrive in St Stanisław Kostka Church, and at 10 p.m. the first Mass for the safe return of Father Jerzy was celebrated there. This Mass marked the beginning of a ten-day-long vigil as people awaited conclusive news of his fate. It continued day and night; many parishioners spent all their free time and every night praying in church. Silent prayers and meditations were frequently interspersed with the celebration of Mass. Every day the rosary was recited aloud and the Stations of the Cross meditated on. At one of these meditations, those following the Stations of the Cross were led by all the professors from the Warsaw Seminary and some three hundred seminarians. The focal point of each day was the evening Mass at seven o'clock, at which thousands of people would gather. It was celebrated by an increasing number of Warsaw's priests and those from other dioceses as well. On 26th October the head of the Roman Catholic Church in Poland, Cardinal Glemp, arrived at the church of St Stanisław Kostka and joined the priests to celebrate Mass. Two days earlier Bishop Zbigniew Kraszewski, the auxiliary bishop of Warsaw, had celebrated the evening Mass for the release of his priest and close friend. In his sermon he described Father Jerzy as "God's Hero", and in a passionate plea asked everyone to pray fervently to God so that He in His mercy would make Father Jerzy's return to them possible. Some friends of Father Jerzy spontaneously organized an information centre, and for the next few days, "every now and then", a communiqué would appear on the parish notice board. It was immediately surrounded by people eager for any news of their missing priest.

People, however, came to St Stanisław Kostka Church mainly to join in the prayers, believing that Father Jerzy "must" return to them. At first their hopes were high. One of Father Popiełuszko's friends even tried to convince the others that Father Jerzy would probably persuade the kidnappers to confess their sins to him, just as he had done with the criminal during his night in prison. Then they would bring him back to the church. But as time passed and there was still no news of Father Jerzy's whereabouts, the fears of the people grew steadily.

On Sunday 21st October, Father Popiełuszko's brother, Stanisław, arrived in Warsaw to pray for him in "his" church. He was to spend the whole of the next week travelling between Warsaw and Okopy, where Father Jerzy's parents were eagerly waiting for any information about him. They had learnt of their son's kidnapping from the television news. They had been alone in the house that evening, as Stanisław and his wife had gone to the church in Suchowola to take part in a special service. As on every other October evening, it being a "Marian month", Father Jerzy's parents had recited the rosary together. Władysław Popiełuszko, feeling very tired, decided to go to bed early but his wife, on a sudden impulse – she who never watched the news – switched on the TV set. The news had begun. Suddenly she heard the name Popiełuszko. As she listened to the communiqué she fell to her knees and began to pray. The following day she tied a red shawl (symbol of martyrdom) over her head, and she wore it until Father Jerzy's body was found. "It seemed to me at the time that he was still alive, being tortured somewhere", she explained later to a visiting priest.

Various groups and individuals, both in Poland and abroad, were voicing their shock and horror at this outrageous crime. Letters of sympathy started to pour into the church of St Stanisław Kostka and into Cardinal Glemp's office. On 21st October Lech Wałesa came to

Father Jerzy's church and publicly warned the perpetrators of this inhuman crime that "If a hair on Father Popiełuszko's head has been harmed – then someone will be taking upon himself a terrible responsibility." On the same day Seweryn Jaworski, vice-chairman of Solidarity in the Warsaw Mazowsze region, issued an appeal for constant prayer and vigil. He also asked that the workers should pray at their places of work for the safe return of Father Jerzy. On 22nd October fifteen intellectuals sent a letter to General Jaruzelski, placing the ultimate blame for the abduction on the authorities: "The campaign pursued by the press against Father Popiełuszko suggests that the kidnapping was a political act. Regardless of who had an interest in this crime, we are convinced that the guilt will rest with the authorities."

At noon on the same day the Warsaw Curia issued its first official statement. It was signed by two auxiliary bishops of Warsaw – Władysław Miziołek and Kazimierz Romaniuk – and by the deputy secretary of the Polish Episcopate, Bishop Jerzy Dabrowski. The bishops appealed to the authorities not only to "undertake all possible action to find Father Popiełuszko" and to explain this shocking assault on innocent people, but also to release Waldemar Chrostowski immediately – he was still being held by the police and refused any contact with his lawyer. He was in fact released the following day and taken to Warsaw in a police convoy. There, in his flat, a few "guardian angels" from the security police were waiting for him, supposedly for his own protection. Mr Chrostowski not surprisingly found it difficult to trust them, and after signing a document releasing them from all responsibility for the safety of his life, left and went straight to the church of St Stanisław Kostka. This was the only place where he really felt safe.

That day the mood in the church was more cheerful. The night before, the ten o'clock news had carried an item reporting that a woman had seen a man who fitted the description of Father Jerzy, getting out of a car in Warsaw in the presence of two other people. Hopes that Father Jerzy was still alive rose again.

On 24th October, during his weekly Wednesday audience at the Vatican, John Paul II read out an extract from the communiqué by the Warsaw Curia. He then expressed his "solidarity with Warsaw's clergy and parishioners in the face of this anti-human act of open violence against a priest . . ." The Pope asked the whole Church to pray for Father Jerzy, and appealed to the consciences of those guilty of the crime to release him.

Later that day, at 7.30 p.m., Polish Television announced that five people had been detained in connection with the kidnapping. They included Grzegorz P. – a member of the Ministry of the Interior. The morning papers of 25th October published news of the temporary detention of "G.P." and two other unnamed persons.

The news was met with dismay and horror. Had Father Popiełuszko become yet another victim of the security police in the painful process of "reintroducing law and order"? This was the question many people asked themselves that morning. However, to all those uncharitable enough to suspect the official involvement of the Ministry of Internal Affairs in the kidnapping, Jerzy Urban – the government spokesman – during a press conference on 25th October, revealed that it was "thanks to the Ministry of Internal Affairs, its organization and its officials . . . its selfless and intensive work that the perpetrators of the crime were so speedily discovered". Nevertheless, some people found it quite hard to believe Mr Urban. There had been too many strange, if not to say suspicious, incidents during this "rigorous investigation". For example, two days after Father Popiełuszko's kidnapping, a policeman came to the church of St Stanisław Kostka and asked for a photograph of Father Jerzy. It was not only the timing which was surprising, but also the request itself. After all, it was common knowledge that Father Popiełuszko's bulky file at the Ministry of the Interior contained many photographs of him. Then there was the police visit to the flat of Barbara Jarmuzynska-Janiszewska, Father Jerzy's doctor. She was asked about Father Jerzy's health and the medicines he was taking, including their dosage. An hour after the police had left, functionaries of the secret police came to see her and she was asked the same questions all over again. On 23rd October the police seemed to be searching not only for Father Jerzy but also for some of his friends, especially for Jerzy Wocial, who had publicly read out Seweryn Jaworski's appeal at Warsaw University. Another of Father Jerzy's friends, Karol Szadurski, was "invited" to a meeting at the police station, but he categorically refused to go. Under the pretext of searching for Father Popiełuszko in Bydgoszcz, Słupsk and Szczecin, people suspected of links with underground Solidarity, as well as former political prisoners, were being questioned. One of them, Wiesław W. in Gniezno, was detained for forty-eight hours. The secret police also visited the flat of a well-known actress, Hanna Skarzanka, a close friend of Father Jerzy. She was not at home; her sister-in-law was in the flat at the time, and was asked whether Father Jerzy had disclosed any travel plans to her. Father Popiełuszko's brother, who was returning home from Germany after the kidnapping, was asked at the border, "Are you returning alone? Where is your brother?", the insinuation being that Father Jerzy was abroad.

Great bitterness was aroused by the numerous cases of police provocation and intimidation of Father Jerzy's friends. At seven o'clock on 22nd October several drunken men tried to "instigate disorder" in front of the church of St Stanisław Kostka. The following day a similar incident occurred. This time there were more drunken men; not far away the militia were waiting, ready to move in "to restore law and order". The same afternoon an explosive device went off just outside the presybtery. On 25th October Krzysztof Wolf and Janusz Sadło, who had organized a prayer meeting for Father Jerzy in the Warsaw steel plant, were interrogated by the secret police. Jozef Kupiec, who had switched off the internal public address system so that the prayers could be recited in peace, was also summoned by the secret police. Another steel worker, a member of St Stanisław Kostka's security service during the Masses for the Country, found a slanderous note pinned on the door of his flat threatening him with death. By an ironical coincidence, on 24th October, when Grzegorz Piotrowski was first detained, the Disciplinary Commission for the civil servants of the Warsaw court demoted Joanna Sokoł from her position as councillor. "On 22nd February 1984 Joanna Sokoł had taken part in a public expression of sympathy and admiration for the then accused Father Popiełuszko, by leaving the building to escort him out of it. This gesture of sympathy towards the person under investigation undermines the authority of a member of the jurisdiction", stated the official verdict.

In this atmosphere of tension, uncertainty and speculation, the identity of the kidnappers was finally released. On 27th October, the day before the planned October Mass for the Country, the Polish people had the extraordinary experience of seeing their Minister for Internal Affairs announcing on television, "with the greatest sorrow", that the perpetrators of the kidnapping of Father Jerzy were three young functionaries of the Ministry of the Interior. Grzegorz Piotrowski, head of a section in one of the departments of the Ministry, was named as chief organizer of the kidnapping. His accomplices and subordinates, Waldemar Chmielewski and Leszek Pekala, were said to have obeyed Piotrowski's orders "in good faith". The Minister condemned this "revolting crime", and assured his audience that its perpetrators would suffer a severe penalty. He also promised that the background of the crime would be explained publicly. Many ordinary Poles were impressed by his solemn, even sad, demeanour, particularly when he talked of the crime being "especially painful to the employers of the Ministry", and when he earnestly appealed for public co-operation in finding Father Jerzy "if he is still alive", he gave an impression of honesty.

This ingenious psychological manoeuvre convinced many, at least for the time being, that on this occasion the authorities were probably innocent. On Sunday 28th October, the Mass for the Country was celebrated without Father Jerzy. Eighty thousand people came to pray for him, with delegations coming from all parts of the country. The previous day General Kiszczak had mentioned that Father Popiełuszko might be dead, and even though the people could not, and did not want to, accept such an unthinkable possibility, the mood was sombre. By this time Masses for the safe return of Father Jerzy were being said in churches throughout Poland. In St Stanisław Kostka Church a special vigil rota was set up. Groups representing various professions, districts of Warsaw and regions of the country were praying for Father Jerzy. The whole of Poland was praying. On the spot where he had been abducted the local scout group made a birch cross and ensured that lamps were burned beside it continuously.

On 29th October the Ministry of the Interior stated that a search for Popiełuszko's body was being carried out in the river Wisła, in the vicinity of Torun, and in the Włocławek reservoir. At eight o'clock the following day, when Mass at St Stanisław Kostka Church had just come to an end, Father Andrzej Przekazinski announced in a voice broken with emotion, "Brothers and sisters, today, in the waters of the Włocławek reservoir, the body of the priest . . ." His words were extinguished by a crescendo of loud cries and wails. People fell to their knees. The priest tried to start up a Lenten hymn but his voice broke. He joined openly in the spontaneous weeping. The church began to fill with people once again. All night, every hour, Mass was celebrated. There were not enough liturgical vestments for all the priests wishing to concelebrate the Mass. Liturgical vestments in red – the colour signifying martyrdom – were used. By midnight, thousands of candles and lamps had been lit and placed alongside the metal fence surrounding the church grounds; the fence itself became barely visible, covered as it was in flowers.

Representatives of the steel workers went to Okopy to bring Father Jerzy's parents back to St Stanisław Kostka Church. The question of his burial place remained open. His body was taken to Białystok for an autopsy, and many began to fear that his parents would be forced to bury their son in his home parish, far away from his workers, his friends and his place of work. When subjected to pressure from the authorities, Marianna Popiełuszko gave one simple reply: "Once I gave my son away to the Church, and I am not going to take him back now." Both parents saw Warsaw – where their son had worked and where he was loved so much – as the only suitable place for his eternal rest. They arrived in Warsaw on 31st October and went straight to the church, where a priest was delivering a sermon. They walked up to the altar, and then suddenly Father Jerzy's father prostrated himself before the altar, and uttered a loud groan. The whole congregation broke into tears at the despair of the father, who then kissed the stones of the floor walked upon by his son's feet. For the next few days he could not stop crying, and had to be almost carried everywhere by the steel workers. Father Jerzy's mother could not cry. It was as if she still could not believe that her son was really dead. At the end of the Mass the priest announced the decision of Father Jerzy's parents that the burial would take place in Warsaw. But the people wanted more. They wanted Father Jerzy to be where they believed his spirit already was – in "his" church of St Stanisław Kostka. Father Popiełuszko's mother also pleaded with Cardinal Glemp that he let their son be buried amongst his parishioners at "his" church.

Far into the night thousands of people queued up to sign a letter to Cardinal Glemp, asking the Cardinal to allow Father Popiełuszko to be buried in the church grounds. The next day the Cardinal changed the decision of the committee responsible for the burial – Father Jerzy would not after all be buried at Powaski cemetery but in the grounds of St Stanisław Kostka Church in Zoliborz.

The burial would be on 3rd November 1984.

On 2nd November, two Warsaw priests, Father Edward Zmijewski and Father Grzegorz Kalwarczyk, arrived in Białystok, to take the body of Father Jerzy back to Warsaw. At 12.50 the closest members of his family, his friend Jacek Lipinski, and Father Cezary Potocki, representing the archdiocese of Białystok, arrived at the institute of forensic medicine, where Father Popiełuszko's body was being kept. The main gate was locked. In front of it was a crowd of people whose numbers continued to increase, despite attempts by the local police to disperse them. An old lady handed one of the priests a bouquet of flowers, which she begged them to take to Father Jerzy. She had already been waiting for over four hours to catch a glimpse of the coffin. After a while, an official promised that the coffin would be allowed to leave by the main gate. The crowd sighed with relief. The three priests and Jacek Lipinski went to identify the body. His parents, at the suggestion of a doctor who was afraid that they might suffer too much of a shock, decided to wait in the chapel.

In a room guarded day and night by four secret policemen, Father Jerzy's body, lying on a metal bed, was covered with white paper. The paper was removed – and they looked with horror at the massacred body, unable to recognize their friend. The whole body was covered in bruises of a brownish grey colour. The face was deformed. The nose and areas around the eyes were black, the fingers were brown and dark red, the feet greyish. His hair was much thinner, as if some of it had been pulled out. Large areas of the skin on his legs seemed to have been torn away. Mr Lipinski decided to check Father Jerzy's teeth. When the mouth was opened, they saw a piece of pulp in the place where the tongue should have been. Then Father Jerzy's brother was called in, and in the end it was he who made the identification from the birth mark on the side of his chest. The nuns now came in and began to dress Father Jerzy for his coffin. Three badges were pinned on his cassock: his favourite – the Black Madonna against a red and white background; a Solidarity badge from the Warsaw steel plant; and a badge with the church of St Stanisław Kostka engraved on it, together with the inscription "Mass for the Country, Warsaw". A wooden cross with the inscription "Solidarity" on both arms, and a rosary given to Father Jerzy by Pope John Paul II were placed in his hands. Finally, his face was powdered to cover at least the terrible black and blue bruising. The coffin was taken to the chapel and Father Popiełuszko's parents came in to see their son.

At three o'clock Edward Kisiel, Bishop of the archdiocese of Białystok, arrived to pray over the coffin; but no one could really pray. They all just stood there weeping, stunned by the sight before them. In the end the coffin was closed. The priests took it on their shoulders and carried it outside. In front of the coffin walked the seminarians and priests, the parents and the Bishop. In the meantime thousands of people had gathered outside the gate, and about two thousand had even managed to get inside the square. From the main gate to the chapel two rows of candles and lamps were burning. The main gate was opened at last and the procession entered the square. The crowd took the coffin and carried it to the hearse. People tried at least to touch the coffin, and many were in tears – including the driver of the hearse.

In the end the hearse managed to drive off, followed by two hundred taxis and many private cars. All of them blew their horns. People were kneeling in the streets as the coffin passed, and lighted candles were placed along the route. The procession also passed eight police check-points, where the policemen were seen noting down the registration numbers of the taxis – some two hundred and twenty were written down in all. At the border of the archdiocese the final farewell was said. Everyone left their cars and knelt as Bishop Kisiel stood beside the coffin. A long silence followed. Then after a short prayer Jacek Lipinski thanked everybody and said, "We are taking Father Jerzy so that he can stay with us for ever." The next day all the taxi drivers who had driven in the procession were summoned to the police station for no specified reason. When only a delegation from the taxi drivers went, they were fined.

After leaving the archdiocese the escort of six cars drove towards Warsaw. Every few kilometres they passed a police patrol, but they were never stopped. When they finally arrived at St Stanisław Kostka Church, they were met by a crowd of tens of thousands of people. Since early morning they had been gathering in front of the church, and by 3 p.m., when the hearse was leaving Białystok for Warsaw, the square in front of the church was already full. Inside at the main altar two huge portraits were displayed: one of Father Jerzy celebrating the Mass for the Country, the other of St George – with the face of Father Jerzy – killing the dragon symbolically painted in red. A meeting of those in charge of organizing the church security men for the funeral next day had just begun. Four hundred and fifty men came forward, but even more were needed. On the right-hand side of the church (looking towards the entrance) the grave lay ready. As the hours passed the temperature dropped and cold winds began to blow, but this did not discourage the people, who just kept on arriving. The square in front of the church was packed, and the crowd was now filling the side streets. All the time fresh bouquets and wreaths were being brought and placed at the foot of the catafalque. In the unending recital of prayers one message recurred again and again – and that was the need to overcome hatred, the need for a moral victory of good over evil.

Weariness began to overcome people, children sat on the ground, someone in the crowd asked for a doctor. Then at 6.30 p.m. the funeral procession arrived. The coffin was carried into the church by Father Jerzy's closest friends. Behind the coffin came his parents. The church bells began to toll. The simple coffin was laid on the catafalque, and Father Jerzy's stole was placed on top of it. At seven o'clock Mass was celebrated as it had been for the last ten days – but this time Father Jerzy was present. After this Mass it was announced that everybody would have a chance to pay their last respects to Father Jerzy. Orderlies at the side entrance asked people not to kneel down or to stop at the coffin . . . tens of thousands of people patiently queued outside. In front of the church a group of men quickly erected a high catafalque, and Father Jerzy's coffin would be placed there in the early morning. At the side of the presbytery candles and lamps were arranged in the form of a cross and a heart. They lit up the inscriptions and farewell notes pinned to the fence: ". . . and forgive us our trespasses, as we forgive those who trespass against us . . ."; a statement from underground Solidarity: "We could not defend the one man who was most dear to us." On the front of the church a huge banner was still hanging: "Wherever you are, Christ and our prayers are with you." Only in the early hours of the morning would it be replaced by the slogan "God – Honour – Country". On the hedge separating the church square from the small garden adjacent to the presbytery another earlier banner was hanging: "God, give us back Father Jerzy."

At the coffin the first guard of honour was mounted. They would change every twenty minutes until morning. On the fence was a notice signed by non-believers, stating that they would be joining in the vigil beside Father Jerzy's coffin. According to those present there was a unique atmosphere that night in the church. It was as if the physical presence of the whole of Poland was there, gathered in solidarity around this one priest. The confessionals were brought out and placed around the church, and soon long queues formed. Midnight arrived and again Mass was celebrated. The whole front of the main altar was overflowing with flowers, and they just kept on arriving. Some were placed beside the metal fence next to huge photographs of Father Jerzy, with the inscription "our chaplain". It was two o'clock in the morning and inside the church many people were falling asleep – among them nurses and orderlies. The actor who had led the church singing for hours on end fell asleep with the Bible under his head: he had spent the last eleven nights in the church.

It was by now bitterly cold. The priests hearing confessions wrapped themselves in blankets. Those kneeling down for confession were also shivering, but the queues were seemingly endless. Some of the confessions had only previously been heard when the confessors first received communion. The priests spoke of many conversions to the faith that night.

At five in the morning everyone was asked to leave the church. Only Father Popieluszko's closest family stayed behind, along with a few priests. The last farewells were said, the coffin was sealed and then it was placed on the raised platform in front of the church. Above it a monumental backcloth, in the form of the red and white Polish flag, hung practically the whole way down the front façade of the church. The red and white parts of the flag were split at the top to form a huge V sign, symbolizing victory. The square in front of the church was almost deserted. Only a few people, the most persevering of those who had come the night before, were still standing outside the front gate, waiting for the funeral, which was due to begin at 11 a.m.

By 7 a.m. the crowds had returned. First the delegations from all over Poland. They had arrived on the overnight trains, and some had marched in columns from the station. Only three people from each delegation were allowed behind the gate. The square and the park beside it quickly filled up with people, and soon newcomers had to be satisfied with standing places in the side streets. People climbed the trees; all overlooking roofs were already occupied. Extracts from Father Jerzy's sermons were read over the loudspeakers. The people listened, repeating together after each reading "Overcome evil with good". Thousands of candles, lamps and flowers were being passed over people's heads towards the church and there handed to the orderlies. Where they would squeeze them in, amongst all the rest, was becoming a major problem.

Father Jerzy's parents were already sitting by the catafalque, praying. Then the Primate of Poland arrived with some of the bishops. The church bells tolled once more. The funeral Mass began, with hundreds of thousands of people repeating loudly three times, "And forgive us our trespasses as we forgive those who trespass against us." The Mass was celebrated by the Primate, with six bishops and six priests, on the church balcony. More than a thousand priests concelebrated inside and outside the church. Beyond the gates to the church stretched an ocean of people – so tightly wedged together that it was difficult for those crying even to wipe away their tears. The crowd was later estimated at between three hundred thousand and three hundred and fifty thousand people. There was an overpowering silence; so solemn was the atmosphere that people present felt as if this was not taking place on earth. One of Father Jerzy's friends later summarized the people's feelings at the Mass: "We knew that he was no longer with us; and even if it was very hard to reconcile ourselves to this fact, we sensed that something so special was happening that it left us no room for despair."

At the end of the Mass the farewell speeches began. The first to speak was Father Ryszard Rumianek, Father Jerzy's friend from his seminary days. Then members of the various communities in which Father Jerzy had carried out his pastoral work took the floor: Andrzej Szczepkowski, a famous actor; Marian Jabłonski, a doctor; Elzbieta Murawska, a nurse; Lech Wałesa, the leader of the banned Solidarity trade union; Father Teofil Bogucki, Father Jerzy's parish priest. The most moving was a short speech by Karol Szadurski, who represented the Warsaw steel plant: He called out: "Jerzy, our friend, you remain with us." Even the toughest of men in the multitude were touched. He continued, "Today all the steel men have come here. There are lads from Gdansk, Piekary Slaskie, Mistrzejowice, Nowa Huta, Czestochowa, Swiebodzin, Zielona Gora, Wrocław, Krakow, from all over Poland.

Father Jerzy, can you hear the tolling bells of freedom? Can you hear our hearts praying? The Pope, the Primate and your parish priest are praying with us. Listen with us and above us. Your ark, the 'Solidarity of hearts', drifts along, carrying more and more of us with it . . . you have already won with Christ . . . and you wanted this victory so much. Jerzy, our chaplain, farewell.''

The coffin was taken from the catafalque and carried in procession to the grave, preceded by the Primate and the bishops, followed by Father Jerzy's family. The bells tolled for the last time. The Primate – Cardinal Jozef Glemp – prayed over the grave surrounded by the banners of several delegations as the coffin was lowered. "God, who has defended Poland", a solemn religious hymn, was sung while all the banners were lowered. The funeral was over.

Soon the grave was sealed, by bricks. Over the coffin was placed a replica of the banner of the Warsaw steel plant. Beside the grave Father Stanisław Małkowski, Father Jerzy's friend, knelt down in prayer. Only a few months later, during the trial of Father Popiełuszko's murderers, Father Małkowski was to learn that, according to their plans, he should have been "silenced" first. If it had not been for Captain Piotrowski's preference, Father Stanisław would now have been lying in the grave, instead of his friend. Beside him two other people were still kneeling – a woman in black and a man in an old fur coat – Jerzy's parents.

Once again people began to form a long queue to file past the grave. Soon it became buried under flowers and wreaths. More candles were lit. By evening the mass of candles and lamps covered almost the whole square in front of the church, as well as the pavements of all the adjacent streets. Thousands were still waiting to pass by Father Jerzy's grave. On the fence a new inscription appeared: "We promise not to abandon the way you showed us, Nowa Huta"; "Do not be afraid of those who kill the body, for even then the spirit remains untouched, Solidarity, Łodz"; "Faithful to the ideals of Father Jerzy"; "You shall always remain our chaplain, Students"; "Solidarity of hearts with Father Jerzy"; "You led us towards love and freedom, Białystok"; and many, many others. But perhaps the most important of all was: "And forgive us our trespasses as we forgive those who trespass against us."

The Christian value of forgiveness did not, however, silence the basic questions being asked by the people: Who were the murderers and on whose orders were they acting? From the beginning, the authorities were wavering between maintaining that this was a "political provocation" against the Polish government by the "hardliners" at the highest level, and the implausible assertion that this was the isolated work of Captain Piotrowski, an exceptionally bad character in an otherwise selfless, dedicated and heroic force.

When the trial opened on 27th October, in the provincial court in Torun, extraordinary security measures, bordering on farce, were taken. From dawn on the day of the trial the courtroom was surrounded by policemen; reinforcements waited in buses parked in side streets, while a helicopter chattered low overhead. To get into Courtroom Number 40 where the trial was held, one not only had to have a special pass, but also to undergo *two* identity checks as well as a body search by the members of the "anti-terrorist" unit. The soldiers even stood at so-called strategic points in the courtroom. It was hard to make out whether these incredible security precautions were to protect the defendants against possible attackers, or whether the authorities feared a public mass storming of the court.

Apart from Piotrowski, Chmielewski and Pekala, one other man was in the dock. He was Colonel Adam Pietruszka, deputy head of the department dealing with the Church within the Ministry of the Interior. During the trial the only other person in authority to testify before the court was Pietruszka's immediate superior, General Płatek, head of the church department. However, the court could not find enough evidence to prove his complicity in the kidnapping of Father Jerzy. General Płatek had already been suspended from his position shortly before Piotrowski's arrest. During the investigation Pekala and Chmielewski mentioned the deputy minister who "gave the order", but in court they both withdrew their statements. The court itself had gone to great lengths to prove that the affair concerned just the four men in the dock.

The judge would cut short any statement which even hinted at anything to the contrary. The Pekala revelation that there had been similar "cases" before fell on the judge's deaf ears. At the end of the trial, the court was to "reassure" the public that if there were any instigators of the crime then they were definitely not within the Polish Ministry of the Interior, or for that matter in any other section of the Polish authorities. One of the state prosecutors even hinted during the trial that, "We still might learn that it was some Western circle, interested in destabilizing the Polish regime, which was behind the kidnapping." At this point relative common sense prevailed and the accusation was not pursued.

The previous devotion to duty and loyalty of all four defendants was repeated throughout the trial. Indeed they had all received state and ministerial medals "in recognition of their work". It was obvious that Piotrowski, the organizer of the murder, was an especially trusted man within the ranks. At the tender age of thirty-three he was already a departmental head of probably the most important and the most sensitive section within the entire Ministry of the Interior. It was Piotrowski, for example, who was chosen to escort the church officials allowed to visit Lech Wałesa when he was "exiled" at the beginning of martial law.

In court Piotrowski behaved arrogantly; he was self-confident and ever ready to contradict the judge when he got any detail wrong. He showed no remorse for killing Father Popiełuszko. At times he displayed some feelings of guilt for implicating his two subordinates, but for Father

Jerzy all he felt was hatred. During the trial, Piotrowski was allowed not to answer questions put forward by the auxiliary prosecutors representing Father Jerzy's family; and he was even encouraged by the judge to indulge in a half-hour burst of hatred towards his victim. It was not only Piotrowski who freely slandered the murdered priest and the Church – the other defendants, the judge, even the prosecutors joined in what was now becoming the posthumous trial of Father Jerzy and the Catholic Church in Poland. Leszek Pietrasinski, the deputy procurator of the Procurator General's Office, went furthest in his shocking and inhuman assault on the murdered priest. In his final speech he called the murderers equal with their victim: "They were guilty of the same crime," he stated, "a provocative attack against the policy of reconciliation and dialogue pursued by the Polish government." By the end of the trial the auxiliary prosecutors, acting on behalf of the family of Father Jerzy, were forced into a position whereby they were effectively acting in the role of defence counsel for the murdered priest.

Piotrowski pleaded not guilty to the killing; he admitted only "the participation in" "certain operations": he "only" hit the priest with the club first, "only" tied and gagged him and "only" dumped the priest into the reservoir. It was the first time that he had hit a man, Piotrowski exclaimed dramatically in court. Yet the doctor who carried out the post mortem revealed to a priest that in his entire career he had never seen a man so badly damaged internally after "only" being beaten up. Piotrowski did not hesitate to claim that were it not for Father Popiełuszko's obstinacy and determination to disobey orders, the killing would not have happened. Many found it almost impossible to comprehend the fact that, right up until the end, there was no visible proof of Piotrowski recognizing that what he had done was morally wrong. Another shocking and revealing statement before the court was the admission by both Pekala and Chmielewski that not only were they absolutely convinced of their impunity, but that they had also hoped to further their professional careers by participating in the crime – and now they felt "cheated".

They had many reasons to believe that they would go unpunished. The Helsinki Watch Group lists some ninety-three known victims of the secret police since 13th December 1981, when martial law was declared. Only in one case was a full investigation ordered. It was after a nineteen-year-old student, Grzegorz Przemyk, died as a result of a "questioning session" with the security police in Warsaw in May 1983. The secret policemen were put on trial. However, despite the full testimony made by the dying victim to a doctor in the Warsaw Hospital, the secret policemen were still found innocent. The court decided that it was the people manning the ambulance which took Grzegorz to the hospital who were guilty of his death.

Why therefore should Father Popiełuszko's murderers fear the court's decision? The answer lies in the words of the deputy prosecutor of the Procurator General's Office in Warsaw: "If the defendants have to be punished then it is not so much because they have killed a man, but mainly because they have smeared the good name of the Ministry." It was difficult not to draw the conclusion that in fact they were punished for incompetence. After all, if Piotrowski's "operational group" had put more thought and care into their assignment, then both Father Popiełuszko and Waldemar Chrostowski would have died in a mysterious accident like others before them – amongst them Kazimierz Kluz, the auxiliary bishop of Gdansk (1982); Father Honoriusz Kowalczyk, a Dominican university chaplain in Poznan (1983); Piotr Bartoszcze (1984); Stanisław Chac (1984); and over ninety others – yet with not enough proof in the eyes of Polish communist law for any conviction, even though the circumstantial evidence was incriminating.

The death sentence demanded in the case of Piotrowski was changed by the procurator to twenty-five years' imprisonment. Pietruszka was also sentenced to twenty-five years, Pekala and Chmielewski to fifteen and fourteen years respectively. As the sentence was conveyed to the people a bitter joke was born and began to circulate in Poland: "Question: Why did Piotrowski get twenty-five years' imprisonment? Answer: One year for killing Father Jerzy and twenty-four for messing it up."

The open trial of secret policemen in a communist country, and the fact that in the end they were found guilty of murdering a Catholic priest, impressed many people in the West. The Poles, however, do not share the enthusiasm of the West for this recent exhibition of Polish communist law. For them the trial left too many questions which will probably never be answered. For example, would the trial ever have taken place if Waldemar Chrostowski had not managed to escape and to make a detailed testimony to a priest before the forces of "law and order" grabbed him? During his short journey in the Fiat, Chrostowski could have recognized at least one of the assailants – Pekala, whom he had met before when he acted as a witness during a search of Father Popiełuszko's flat in which Pekala took part.

In answer to the question "Who ordered the murder of Father Popiełuszko?" it is quite clear to any careful observer of the trial that, by its very nature, the way it functioned, the overwhelming tendencies that dominated it and of course the known hard facts, the order came from higher up than Pietruszka. This in itself casts doubts on the legitimacy of the trial as such.

What is most important to the Poles is the fact that the murderers of all the other victims of martial law – including Stanisław Chac, who was kidnapped and tortured on the same day as Father Jerzy – are still free and will probably never be brought to trial. What really worries the Poles is that since Father Popiełuszko's murder, two more priests, Father Kosciołko and Father Ziomek, were both tortured by "unknown hooligans" in the region of Lublin. This time the selfless secret police somehow did not manage to track down the assailants. Another priest, Father Rufin

Abramek, a Pauline monk from the monastery at Czestochowa, was almost killed and left badly injured in another mysterious road accident. The car in which he was travelling was hit by a heavy lorry after the driver had ignored a stop sign at a road junction. Although all his particulars were taken down by the police, so far they have not brought any proceedings against the "careless driver".

Who will ever be able to verify independently whether the four found guilty of Father Jerzy's murder will actually serve their sentences, or whether they will be quietly granted an amnesty?

# Epilogue

". . . unless a wheat grain falls on the ground and dies . . ."

"I tell you most solemnly, unless a grain of wheat falls on the ground and dies, it remains only a single grain; but if it dies it yields a rich harvest." (John 12:24)

Christ once said, as He stood before Pilate, "For this I came into the world to bear witness to the truth." For preaching the truth He was repaid by crucifixion. Could Father Jerzy – a faithful disciple of Christ – have expected any better than his master? Like Christ, Father Jerzy was innocent but still accused, treacherously captured, severely beaten and in the end suffered his own "crucifixion". Like those who crucified Christ, the murderers of Father Popiełuszko were convinced that by killing him they had "solved the problem", that their action would silence the troublemakers, not realizing that love and truth can be crucified but never killed. Blinded by Satan's hatred they could not see that the inhuman killing of a young and courageous priest would place Father Jerzy Popiełuszko among Christ's triumphant martyrs, for he had followed his master all the way up to Calvary. Father Jerzy's mother has always been convinced that her son's death was "the will of God". A young Polish Catholic intellectual recently described it as "an act of God's Providence".

Since 13th December 1981, when the Polish authorities declared war on their own citizens, the list of victims either killed or injured has grown slowly but steadily, amidst the passivity of the people at large. This state of terror in the eighties, with victims counted "only" in their tens, seems to many a positive improvement in comparison with the period between 1944 and 1948, when some thirty thousand people vanished without trace during the consolidation of communist authority in Poland. Even in the early 1950s, people were condemned with the full weight of the law and then executed, simply as a result of an anonymous telephone call or a letter informing the authorities of the victim's "political unsoundness". Membership of the Polish Home Army (AK) Underground Resistance, which took its orders from the "bourgeois" Polish government in exile based in London, was also punishable by death.

The virtually public killing of a Catholic priest – who had courageously and uncompromisingly followed his vocation and preached nothing but love and forgiveness – by members of the security police was probably the greatest personal shock to the Polish people in their post-war history. Many now admit that it was Father Jerzy's cruel death which made them realize, more than ever before, the evil of the system, with its ideology of confrontation, hatred and contempt for man.

Father Popiełuszko's death has already resulted in the return to God of many prodigal sons and daughters. Not so long ago Marianna Popiełuszko, Father Jerzy's mother, whilst walking in Warsaw, overheard a conversation between two women. One of them was saying that she had somehow felt compelled to visit the grave of Father Jerzy day after day. She would just stand at the grave of the murdered priest, not quite sure why she was there. Then one day, whilst standing at the grave, she started to look at her own life and saw how far she had drifted away from her Christian faith. On impulse she went to confession – for the first time in years. "I never felt happier in my life", she said. "Now I shall never stop visiting Father Jerzy's grave, to thank him for changing my life."

People from all over Poland come to pray at Father Popiełuszko's grave and to participate in the Mass that is still said for him in his church every evening at seven o'clock. Among the huge crowds of believers there are always delegations from various factories and regions. Close by, day and night, representatives of the Warsaw steel plant stand guard. At the spot where a memorial will soon be erected there lies a mound of flowers, a cross and a plaque bearing an inscription in which the word "Patron" is used. This term is generally applied to a saint, but even at this early stage its use surprises no one.

It is now, after his death, that Father Jerzy presents a much greater threat and is far more dangerous to the Polish communist authorities than he ever was before. Whilst he was alive they could always hope that their intimidation would silence him. Now in glory he inspires his people and proves to them that a man is free if he bears witness to the truth.

Father Popiełuszko's spirit, his teaching, the testimony of his life and the challenge of his death will remain for ever with the Polish people. At the funeral, and speaking on behalf of all Poles, Lech Wałesa, the leader of the banned Solidarity trade union, made a promise to Father Jerzy, "not to wilt in the face of violence, to respond to lies with the truth and to build a civilization of love". The death of Father Jerzy made the Polish people realize, more than ever before, that the only way to acquire freedom is through a spiritual revolution – a renewal of every individual so that an inner independence of mind and spirit is acquired and manifests itself outwardly.

Can this spiritual revolution, which began in August 1980, succeed against the evil machinery of the totalitarian state? Certainly Father Jerzy has won a decisive battle in its favour. In answer to this question, someone reminded the author of what André Malraux had once said: the twenty-first century will be religious or not be at all. Is there any other way, not only for the Poles, but for all of us?

# Memories of Father Jerzy Popiełuszko

ROMAN GULBINOWICZ
*(Metropolitan Archbishop of Wrocław)*

Father Jerzy Popiełuszko was a priest who served God and man as well as he could; he was convinced of the purity of his service. How mysterious is this Polish land! In every epoch it produces countless followers of Christ, and among them new martyrs. In 1979 the Poles celebrated the nine hundredth anniversary of the death of St Stanisław – a martyr for the right way of life among the people of Poland. 1982 was the year of Maximilian Kolbe – a martyr for the love of his fellow beings. Now the murdered Father Popiełuszko is already described by many as a martyr for the truth. Because of his adherence to the truth, Father Popiełuszko lost his life. He hardly ever spoke of himself, but when he did he used to say: "My work is of a religious and not of a political nature. The proof of this are the crowds of workers who fill the churches. Many of them had not been to church for a long time. Today they attend regularly."

As their chaplain he struggled, together with the Warsaw steel men, for the right to freedom; he accepted the ideal of the independent free trade union "Solidarity" as his own. This should not surprise us. For this ideal stems largely from the truth of the Gospel. He accepted this truth long before 1984, as a child in his family, then at school, and eventually in the Warsaw Seminary. When he was ordained this truth was given to him as a mission he must fulfil.

Father Popiełuszko said to his closest friends: "They

want me to keep silent", but he felt in himself the strength and the need to preach Christ's truth. There is a scene in the Bible when Jesus triumphantly enters Jerusalem on Palm Sunday. Whilst His disciples were shouting: "Blessings to the King who comes in the name of the Lord!", those who were jealous, the Pharisees, turned to Jesus and told Him: "Master, check your disciples." Christ answered them: "I tell you, if these keep silence the very stones will cry out." As he went about his pastoral work, Father Popiełuszko was convinced by the voice of his conscience that he must not fall silent.

There is a beautiful custom in the region where Father Jerzy comes from. When the coffin containing the body of a dead man is being taken to the cemetery, at the cross which always stands on the outskirts of the village the coffin is set down in the middle of the road and the oldest member of the community thanks the dead person for all the good he has done in his life for his family and neighbours . . . Let us then thank Father Jerzy for all the good he has done as a son, as a pupil, as a seminarian and as a priest. We want to thank you, Father Jerzy, for your faithfulness to the truth, for your courage in witnessing to it. This witness was central not only for yourself but for all who came to hear you preach.

I knew Father Jerzy since his early years in the seminary, and I can say without hesitation that he never saw himself as a politician; he was a quiet and modest man. But always I saw in him this attachment to the truth he believed in, the truth he carried in his heart and in his thoughts, the truth he witnessed to during his entire life. When we look today at the life and death of Father Jerzy Popiełuszko one thought comes to our minds: what strength God gives to those who really want to follow Him: most importantly Father Popiełuszko left us a model of a Christian life in our difficult times, a model for which we shall always be thankful. (St Ann's Church, Vatican City, 31st October 1984)

## *A Martyr for the Truth*

FATHER ADAM BONIECKI
*(Editor of the Polish edition of* L'Osservatore Romano*)*

We met twice. On the first occasion we had to break off our conversation after four or five hours . . . and yet my feeling was that we had established a rapport. I know he also felt this, for he spoke of it to friends, and mentioned it in the last two sentences of a letter dealing with another matter. Many people today talk of the bond they felt with Father Popiełuszko, he had a gift for establishing such bonds. After his death I thought much about our meetings and about him. Where did his secret lie? Was it in the fact that he was a man of great humility?

We met at the end of 1982 and at the beginning of 1983. He was one of the best-known people in Warsaw, and indeed in Poland, but I couldn't see in him the slightest trace of condescension, self-importance or vanity. He seemed almost taken aback by the fact that he now found himself at the centre of things. He carried out the tasks assigned to him by his superiors, and devoted himself to the service of others. This was his life.

When the Primate entrusted him with the care of the striking steel workers he tried to serve them as best he could. Today everyone knows about the "Masses for the Country", about the addresses, the crowds. It is surely unheard of that a priest should attract so many workers around a pulpit and around an altar. When he spoke of the Masses he barely mentioned the crowds. He spoke rather of the conversions, the cases of people turning back to God. He heard confessions, visited the sick, blessed marriages, baptized. He spoke to me of his happiness, of the joy he experienced as a priest.

But this priestly joy involved at the same time both effort and exhaustion, a constant living for others. In his room, where things lay scattered about and visitors acted as hosts, two things struck one: that he had no time to spend living in it, and that he had many friends. Proof of this were the innumerable gifts – needlework, sculptures, pictures, emblems, sacramentals – some beautiful, some kitsch, which filled every corner of the room. I was told he hardly ever ate. He didn't have time to come to the meals which the priests had together; perhaps he never felt hungry. This was not all. He knew that he might have to pay a high price for what he was doing and saying. The steel workers also knew this. They once said to him, "Father, you are not a private individual, you are a popular 'cause'." He was reconciled with the fact that he had become a public "cause", and that a bodyguard had been organized for him – and that was the way he lived. His room was at first-floor level – once a brick with explosives attached to it had even been thrown through his window. Friends told him, "Jerzy, be careful, something could happen to you!" His answer is remembered word for word – I was particularly asked to note it down: "The most they can do is to kill me. I do not have a wife and children, so no one else can be hurt, and if I am killed what will it have been for? For what I work for. Could there be anything more beautiful?" This was not empty rhetoric. After his death it transpired that he had left a series of very precise directions in case he should die. He knew.

Was he not frightened? Did he provoke danger? I remember my surprise when, as he described his recent arrest, I heard him admit that he feared imprisonment, for without his medicines and his diet he would become ill immediately. And yet he carried on. He had many opportunities to back out. There were even those who expected him to resign, for a variety of laudable reasons. He told them, "That would be a betrayal of all these people. I cannot resign alone."

All that has happened since then distinguishes him so sharply from other men that it would be easy to forget what a cheerful person he was. He talked with amusement of the ways he had found of deceiving the agents-provocateurs who attended his Masses for the Country in sizeable numbers. On the one hand the heavy machine of thick-skinned provocation, and on the other the amusement and glee of the priest. It reminded one of the battle constantly waged between truth and deception: the latter heavy and difficult to construct, while truth, like a spring breeze, melts away the expanses of dirty snow.

When he spoke of the famous addresses which he prepared in hiding, away from the many who constantly demanded his time and attention, he would say that he simply tried to consider again what had already been said by the Pope, by Cardinal Wyszynski, and by the Primate, Cardinal Glemp.

He spoke with warmth of the inmates who shared his prison cell, as he would of friends. They had actually shown him a great deal of respect and sympathy. He promised the militiaman who carried out the humiliating body search (at which even the official was embarrassed) that he would baptize the child which his wife was expecting. I don't know whether in the event time did not run out on that.

He spoke with amusement of the woman prosecutor who tried to draw out interrogation proceedings until she received the expected telephone call confirming that his flat had been "prepared" for a search to be carried out.

Since he himself wished everyone well and was amenable to new friendships, he suffered when those from whom he had a right to expect understanding and support, appeared either not to understand him or to take his intentions amiss. When he spoke of this tears would well up in his eyes.

This is how I remember him, but not quite – for there was something which one cannot describe in words. Perhaps it was this bond. Later I met many people who spoke of his going as they would about someone very close to them. They simply knew him from the church, from his homilies, and they had seen him only from afar.

As I stood among the people at his grave on the night of Christmas Eve, I found myself wondering what meaning this death already had, what meaning it will come to have. I thought that from now on no priest in Poland, no believing Christian, will be able to live as though Father Popiełuszko had not existed, or as though his testimony did not exist. I thought that Father Popiełuszko, who had not desired it, would now and for ever be found in the hearts of all people and at the heart of the most significant events.

WOJCIECK BAKOWSKI
*(A Polish doctor, one of Father Jerzy's medical students)*

Father Jerzy Popiełuszko was the first person I bumped into at Warsaw University's church of St Anna. I had just arrived in Warsaw to study medicine, and was desperately trying to find accommodation. Like many other students, I hoped to find help at the university chaplaincy. From the moment of our first meeting, I decided that I liked Father Jerzy a lot. There was something about him – maybe the fact that he looked like a student or his directness. I still remember that he wasn't wearing a cassock, but he was wearing red socks. We were strangers, yet Father Jerzy seemed to grasp all my problems immediately, despite the fact that, as usual, I explained things badly. Later, I often took part in the Mass at St Anna on a Sunday evening, which he often celebrated. His voice – warm, delicate and balanced – and even more, the way that he celebrated and really experienced the Mass, are still vivid in my memory.

In January 1980, when I had settled down in the Medical Academy, I decided to take part in the regular meetings organized at St Anna's church. To my joy I discovered that Father Jerzy was in charge of the "medical group". Soon I joined the circle of Father Jerzy's student friends. We used to call him "the Boss". We thought it was less embarrassing for him when we talked in the streets or popped out for a portion of chips, but at the same time it still allowed us to uphold the important distance between him, our spiritual father, and us, his students. It was thanks to the lectures organized by Father Jerzy that I realized the sanctity of life, and I clearly saw all the responsibilities I would have as a doctor for the health and life of my future patients. I also began to solve many of my religious and moral problems in the light of the Gospel. After every lecture there was a discussion – often a stormy one – which Father Jerzy chaired wisely and tactfully. He would always steer any discussion in the proper direction.

On the first Friday of every month he celebrated Mass for us. Before communion he would come to each one of us and, shaking our hands firmly but warmly and looking right into our eyes, he would say: "Peace be with you" . . . This Mass was a unique experience for me, and I often thought that the Eucharist of the First Christians must have resembled our Masses. I felt in real communion with God and with the people, not only those present in the church but with all Christians.

At the end of May 1980 Father Jerzy became a resident priest of St Stanisław Kostka, and our "medical group" followed him. One evening in May we were walking just outside the church when Father Jerzy turned to me and said that now, as resident priest, he hoped to rest more and to spend more time with us. In September of that year our "medical group" went with him on a short trip to the Polish Tatra mountains. This was probably the best holiday of my life. Apart from one day when Father Jerzy did not feel well, he took part in all our activities: walking, climbing, singing, joking. Every day there was also, however, time for meditation and prayer – both individual and in a group. We finished every day with a prayer. We gathered in one room, knelt down and, in the light of the candles, we thanked God for His blessings.

1981 brought student strikes in January and February, November and December. Father Jerzy took pastoral care of the striking students at the Medical Academy and at the College for Firemen. He was not only with the students; he also defended them publicly from the pulpit of St Stanisław Kostka Church against the slanders of the Polish mass media. I myself witnessed some of the conversions made during the strikes. They were brought about by Father Jerzy's steadfast witness to the truth. Above all he moved everyone, even staunch atheists, with his readiness to be with the people in all circumstances – he was a true shepherd of his flock. His actions during the strikes brought many students to the chaplaincy when they were over.

Father Jerzy was always interested in our living conditions and our problems. I sometimes thought that he worried more about me than I did myself. He was always ready to offer advice or help, but he respected the individual's right to the final decision. I didn't always listen to his advice, and I knew that he would try to help me in the only way left – he prayed for me.

When the tragic December of 1981 came he remained with those who were deprived of freedom and gave them encouragement and consolation. It was his pastoral work after 13th December that led him to martyrdom. He fulfilled Christ's command to the letter: "There is no greater love than to give one's life for one's fellow man." What happened on 19th October 1984 was a natural consequence of the choice he made on 13th December 1981.

I shall never forget his answer to my concerned reproach that he should not condemn evil in its "institutionalized forms". He answered that if there is just one person who, after participating in a Mass for the Country, finds it easier to face the next day, this will be his greatest reward. "For this alone it is worth taking the risk", he replied. He thought of himself as a poor preacher; every time he stood before the congregation he was nervous and anxious, and spoke with great humility. During the period of his interrogations in 1984 I once tried to cheer him up by saying that the nuns were constantly praying for him. He looked at me and said: "It is also possible that it is the will of God that I should suffer."

It is strange, but the incident of 13th October [when a man tried to cause Father Jerzy's car to crash by throwing something heavy at it] did not arouse our concern for his safety. The next day, he celebrated Mass for the medical community, and this was followed by tea for the students. He talked calmly of the recent attacks on him in the press. On 18th October we went to visit Father Teofil Bogucki in the hospital. In the evening Father Jerzy celebrated Mass. I was there. In the sacristy he mentioned in passing that a day or two earlier he had been to confession. This was my last meeting with Father Jerzy – my dear friend, chaplain, teacher, my "boss".

Now, after his death, I see my "boss" more and more through the eyes of this enormous crowd of people who gathered at his funeral. I feel ashamed that I did not recognize his greatness while he was alive, that now it is these thousands of people, who probably never even met him, who have taught me who Father Jerzy really was.

### N.N.
*(A Polish friend of Father Jerzy's)*

Father Jerzy used to say that he was prepared for anything. Did anybody, including himself, really think that it would come to this?

The news of his brutal murder shocked the world. Many newspapers published a photograph of Father Jerzy showing this boyish figure of a priest with an expression of a very special kind of peace on his face – a peace not of this world. Weak in body but steadfast in spirit, Father Jerzy had fought for truth and justice in the country which he loved so dearly. His only weapon had been prayer, and his "leader" was Christ Himself. Through his martyrdom he suddenly came close to people who had never met him. What can I say, I who had the privilege of being his friend? Goodness radiated from him during all our conversations together. He always defended everyone; he never asked for anything for himself. He was always giving, always serving others – the sick, the poor, the old, doctors, nurses, students, workers. Through his pastoral work and through the Masses for the Country Father Jerzy led a spiritual revolution and the renewal of a sense of the worth of the individual in Poland – both things forming the core of Solidarity, a movement which calls for an inner freedom of mind and spirit as well as for an outer manifestation of these qualities.

Father Jerzy, we now stand over your grave in mourning. I pray that we may never forget your goodness, your faith, your determination to bear witness to the truth – that we may truly build a solidarity of hearts among us.

## CHRIS LANGDON
*(A journalist with London Weekend Television)*

I met Father Popiełuszko only briefly, nearly two years ago, but I can still remember it as if it were yesterday. I went to visit him because of his reputation, which had already spread throughout Poland and beyond, because of his work for the victims of martial law, and also because of the monthly Masses for the Country, through which he was popularly known as "the Solidarity priest".

He was out when I arrived at his home, a tiny first-floor flat in the church buildings by the side of the church of St Stanisław Kostka. From the moment I arrived it was clear from everyone I met that there was something special about Father Popiełuszko. I was told that he was expecting me by the parish worker, a middle-aged man who was obviously devoted to him. I was introduced to Father Bogucki, the parish priest, a tall elderly man, who seemed a bit daunting at first, like many Polish priests of his generation. We tried to communicate, me in my pidgin-Polish, and even then the fatherly protectiveness that he felt towards Father Popiełuszko was abundantly clear.

When Father Popiełuszko returned, after some minutes, the immediate impression I had of him was of someone working to the limits of his physical and emotional endurance. He was thin and looked gaunt. At first he was tense and nervous. It must be said that, as a Western journalist, I was adding to the pressures on him. The deep shadows round his eyes showed how very tired he was. But it was equally obvious that he had a great inner strength, whatever his outward physical frailty. It showed in his eyes; they were remarkable, I find it hard to explain exactly why.

It was probably because they seemed to reveal a sincerity and a determination to carry on, regardless of the personal cost. It was early in the morning, but he had obviously been up for hours, though only now did he have time to snatch some breakfast (some stale cake and coffee substitute) as we talked. He spoke pretty good English. I knew that he had had little opportunity to sleep, since his message that I could visit him had come only at three o'clock that morning. He explained that some parishioners had had problems with the police during the night and he had had to go out and help. Every few minutes one of the parish workers would come in and they would go off to discuss some urgent problem.

Further evidence that I was talking to someone remarkable came from the tiny flat itself. Every inch of wall space was filled, even the bookcases and doors were covered with every possible type of Solidarity poster, pictures of Lech Wałesa, and underground Solidarity graphics. A large map of Poland in red and white, the national colours, was propped up in the adjoining room. It showed every internment camp and prison holding political prisoners in Poland. The total effect of all these displays seemed quite astounding compared to what I had seen elsewhere in Poland; even Solidarity sympathizers would only cautiously reveal to me their underground Solidarity material, hidden rather than being blatantly on display as it was in Father Popiełuszko's flat. At the time it seemed quite astonishing.

It was clear from our conversations that Father Popiełuszko felt that the authorities were deliberately putting pressure on him. He told me in confidence that an incendiary device had been thrown through the window under which we were now sitting, on the night of 13th December 1982, the first anniversary of the imposition of martial law. He was in the adjoining bedroom at the time. He was convinced it had been officially inspired. Through the window, which was now protected with a wire grille, he pointed out the spots where cars of secret policemen watching the church would park on each side of the square onto which the church faces. He told me that he was tailed by one or more cars wherever he drove. He seemed to believe that it wasn't so much to keep watch on him as to intimidate him. His car had been smeared with white paint on a couple of occasions, he said, adding that as cars parked outside the church often got flat tyres, I should watch mine. The only bit of harassment that he really expressed emotion over was the systematic defacement by the secret police of the posters commemorating the death of Grzegorz Przemyk – the young schoolboy who died after a beating in police custody – which were posted by the church entrance gates. He minimized the pressures on himself by laughing at them. He had a delightful boyish sense of fun, which he used to defuse tension.

He told me with some delight, and with his tongue in his cheek, about how the church stewards, or "church militia" as he called them, had developed methods of detecting the secret policemen who watched him during services: they stood near anybody who didn't seem to know the words of the hymns and liturgies, and if they really didn't they would be thrown out! He had a great sense of humour, which he used to ease tension within himself. As we talked he would break off and play with his mischievous little black puppy called Tiny, who he referred to jokingly as his "secret policeman". Tiny chewed trouser legs and shoelaces with gusto, so our conversations were often interrupted with Father Popiełuszko saying "Tiny, stop!" and laughing at the puppy's antics.

When he was talking of his work, nothing would distract him. Again, it was his eyes which said almost as much as his words. I can still remember them. When speaking of his mission, he didn't so much talk as orate. He didn't so much sit as pose. But as he had great charisma he didn't seem at all false. His whole manner was calm and deliberate and calculated. He knew exactly what he was doing, and the consequences. He appeared very calm and self-collected and completely sure of himself.

The thing that made Father Popiełuszko really stand out in my mind was the way he officiated at one of his Masses for the Country held on the last Sunday of May. Tens of thousands of people from all over Poland packed into the church, its grounds and the surrounding streets. It was a remarkable experience. It wasn't that Father Popiełuszko said anything unexpected, it was just that in his sermons he put into words what all those who attended really felt. The service seemed to allow people an opportunity to express together their feelings, to pour out their sorrow and anguish. Father Popiełuszko's sermon was delivered in calm, calculated, measured tones which seemed sometimes to be full of sorrow and at others to be full of controlled anger. To hear him speak was a deeply moving experience. He began by saying, on the night I was there in May 1983, "There have been many tears over the last year and a half since the infamous December night of 1981. Many tears and much suffering. A year ago in the month of May, the month that is dedicated to the Virgin Mary, we spoke here, here in this church, just as a new wave of suffering, sorrow and tears swept our country. But we had hoped that maybe, after all, we would be able to see a brighter future."

The sight of Father Popiełuszko and thousands of people holding small crosses into the air, many of them with tears in their eyes, was an extraordinary experience I shall never forget.


STEFAN FRANKIEWICZ
*(Editor of the Catholic monthly* Wiez, *"The Link")*

I met Father Popiełuszko during an extremely difficult period; it was a few days after the delivery of the charge against him. From our conversation, which lasted many hours, I remember in particular the great peace of mind and even cheerfulness with which he spoke about others and about himself. He spoke about his work. He spoke of the conversions, the returns to the Church which had come about, often after many years of absence or of hostility. He spoke about the letters he received, in which people thanked him for the faith in human nature they had regained. He was deeply convinced of the rightness and of the importance of what he was doing. At one point he asked me, a layman, to glance through the texts of his homilies, and to tell him quite honestly whether there was even the slightest trace of "politicizing", or whether they contained only the teaching of the truths of the Gospel and of principles derived from the Gospel. He regarded himself as a "shepherd of souls" and not a political activist.

After I had left his flat, when he saw vehicles he suspected moving off to shadow me, Father Popiełuszko decided to give me a lift home in his car. As we tried desperately to lose them around the streets of the Zoliborz area of Warsaw, he did not utter a word. He sat concentrated, without any sign of fear, as if engrossed in prayer. (An extract from a broadcast on Radio Vatican, 22nd October 1984)


H. SRZEDNICKA
*(Of Polish parentage, she is very involved in Polish émigré life in Britain)*

I first met Father Jerzy in Warsaw in March 1984, when I arrived as an escort for a medical aid lorry. He was involved in the distribution of medicines and other supplies, and a meeting was arranged for me to see him privately in his parish quarters. Having not the slightest idea of what to expect, and being somewhat tired after several days' activity in Warsaw, the impression he made was all the more vivid. Father Jerzy was undeniably handsome, aesthetically pleasing, a man of immense ·warmth and personal charm, of great energy and vitality, strong – if his handshake is anything to judge by – and completely disarming. His eyes compelled one to absolute honesty; to reveal and express what up to then would have seemed impossible to put into words.

After expressing his thanks for the medical supplies he asked: "Do they still remember me, think about me in

England?" He then added that whenever he was having problems with the authorities or was imprisoned and unaware of what the outcome would be, it gave him great strength and hope that there were people "even in faraway England who think about me, pray for me".

We talked about his experiences in prison and the constant provocations he was subject to, the assaults on his person, the uncertainty of not knowing what the next harassment would be. Characteristic of his absolute belief in the goodness and value of every individual was his reaction to those who persecuted him. "How can they do all this to me? It is so unnecessary, such a nuisance, when I am only trying to do my job, to do what the people want me to do and ask me to do." He further explained this by saying that he would continue the Masses for the Country as long as the people needed them. He spoke with great joy and ardent enthusiasm about those Masses, where thousands were united in common prayer for a free Poland, and how his task was to represent them as best he could. He showed me the stacks of printed sermons awaiting distribution, and seemed sorry that I was leaving Poland the next morning – the last Sunday of the month – and would not be able to attend the Mass that evening. However, I promised to attend such a Mass in the future if the opportunity ever arose.

In late August this same year I returned to Poland for a private visit, and on Sunday 26th August I found myself, with many thousands of others, outside the church of St Stanisław Kostka at 7 p.m. It was an idyllic Warsaw evening, warm, with a slight breeze after the oppressive heat of the day, blue sky, clouds, the lot. An admirable stage for the drama of the Mass that was being held that night. This was the last Mass for the Country that Father Jerzy held and during which he preached. I saw him a few days later. Five months had elapsed since my last visit. Father Jerzy looked distinctly tired as a result of increased harassment, and he no longer looked so happy as on previous occasions. He spoke of how important to him personally the Masses for the Country were, how they filled a need in the nation's soul and at the same time gave him renewed strength, how he was only saying what everyone in the country thought, and how his sermons were built around comments and statements made to him by his faithful. He asked how things were in England, mentioned with gratitude the media's attention to him, and was deeply saddened by what he saw as the West's incomprehension of the issues at stake in Poland. He had just seen some Western journalists and was amazed at how little they had grasped of the lawlessness and brutality of the prevailing system. His final words virtually summarized what was essential to his ministry as a priest: nothing gave him more joy than when, as a result of his teaching, people were converted to belief. All we can do, he added, is to continue to hope and to pray.

I consider it a privilege to have known Father Jerzy, he was a lovely man – or in the words of my seven-year-old son, who also wants a say in the matter: "He was good and holy, he did not harm anybody, he had a good heart, he liked people and he loved God very much. He had a nice dog."

MARY CRAIG
*(British journalist and author)*

I think that I shall always regret not having known Jerzy Popiełuszko better. Even two brief meetings made it impossible for me to get him out of my mind. In the plane next day, en route for England, the overwhelming sorrow I felt was due in large part to my recollections of those meetings.

They had happened by accident. Father Popiełuszko was a name to me, no more, one of many involved in relief work for internees' families or men on the run from the police in post-martial law Poland. With a friend I had gone in October 1983 to the "Solidarity" church of St Stanisław Kostka in Zoliborz, more out of curiosity than anything else, and it was with some surprise that I found myself entering the clergy house next door, past the scrutiny of someone who was obviously a bodyguard. The curate, Father Jerzy Popiełuszko, it seemed, was in need of protection.

We were taken inside, into a room packed with memories of Solidarity – flags, banners, a cross draped with patriotic ribbon and inscribed Bedziemy; another sculpted for him in coal by miners; a plastic model of the three giant crosses in Gdansk which commemorated the murder of the dockyard workers in December 1970.

Suddenly a small, slight, boyish young man in clerical collar and soutane was in the room, talking rapidly and excitedly about Lech Wałesa. Wałesa's Nobel Prize had been announced a few days earlier, amid official disapproval and public (or rather, private) rejoicing. The parish of St Stanisław Kostka had sent its congratulations. It was, said the young priest – who turned out, of course, to be Father Jerzy – a prize not just for Wałesa but for the whole Solidarity movement, and for a nation which had tried to find its salvation without shedding blood. He turned to me: "Do you understand?" he asked. "In all the time of Solidarnosc, not one life was lost. We are very proud of that record of non-violence."

Pausing only to explain that he was rushing off just then to preach in the church, and to invite us to return next evening, he was gone, leaving me intrigued and wanting to know more about him.

So when I returned, on the dot of my appointment with him next evening, it was late and he was tired. In fact, his face was sallow with exhaustion, illness and overwork. He sat down, wrapped his arms lovingly round his dog, and waited for my questions. Tension was obvious in a constantly twitching neck-muscle. "Do you ever relax?" I asked feebly. "Hardly at all", he said. "The only free moments I have are just before getting into bed, on my knees before God, and with no one else in sight." At present he was living in hourly expectation of arrest; a well-wisher had warned him of a new case being prepared against him, based on serious charges of "abusing the freedom of conscience obtaining in the Polish People's Republic". The ludicrous nature of the charge brought a momentary smile to his face, illuminating and transforming it, accentuating his boyishness. "Whatever happens," he said philosophically, "we can only put ourselves in God's hands and trust in the prayers of our friends. They even say I sing seditious hymns," he grinned, "but I say they're just good Marian ones."

I asked him then if he was afraid. "Well, on one level, the purely human one, yes, I'm afraid, but if you believe in Christ, then you know that there is a dimension beyond fear. Arrest, torture, even death itself are not the end of the story." As a celibate priest, with no family to protect, he was essentially free; and he intended to go on using his freedom in defence of the helpless, constantly reiterating that every human being had the right to respect his own conscience. Anyway, he added, that was his own particular pastoral work; from all over Poland now people were writing to thank him for speaking out, for counselling them against cynicism and hatred; asking to be baptized or to make their confession after ten, twenty, thirty, even forty years away from the Church. "How could the Church betray such people?" he asked. "How could I betray them? I must go on speaking for them."

The danger was apparent. If they came to arrest him, what then? "The people will go on praying for me", he smiled. "You see, I may be afraid, but I really have no alternative. I could not act otherwise. Besides, I would only be truly afraid if what I was doing was wrong."

"Well," I persisted, feeling the question was melodramatic, but somehow unavoidable, "is your life in danger?" He didn't even blink. "Of course, yes", he shrugged. "I've always had to live with that risk. But if I must die violently, then I'd prefer to meet death while defending something worthwhile, than save my life by refusing to take a stand against injustice."

There was really nothing to say after that. As I rose to go, he gave me some photographs and a cassette of his sermons. "I have nothing to hide", he said. "If they arrest me and put false words in my mouth, I want you to listen to these sermons and know the truth. Will you speak for me in England, and tell people that I have only ever stated the truth?"

Almost as an afterthought, he took down from the shelf the plastic model of the Gdansk monument. "God bless you", he said, thrusting it into my hand. "Take it to remember me by." "God bless *you*", I muttered, almost in tears and quite bereft of words.

"That man is another Maximilian Kolbe", I blurted out to my friend as we reached the street. She winced. "Yes," she said, "that's what we're all afraid of. But, dear God, not yet, don't let him be a martyr yet. We can't afford to lose him . . ."